Electronic Day Traders' Secrets

Learn from the Best of the Best Day Traders

Marc Friedfertig and George West

with Jonathan Burton

McGraw-Hill

New York   San Francisco   Washington, D.C.   Auckland   Bogotá
Caracas   Lisbon   London   Madrid   Mexico City   Milan
Montreal   New Delhi   San Juan   Singapore
Sydney   Tokyo   Toronto

Library of Congress Cataloging-in-Publication Data

Friedfertig, Marc.

   Electronic day traders' secrets / by Marc Friedfertig and George West.

      p.   cm.

   ISBN 0-07-134767-4

   1. Electronic trading of securities.   I. West, George.

II. Title.

HG4515.95.F743   1999

332.64'Q285—dc21   99-18007

                                                                                                        CIP

McGraw-Hill

A Division of The McGraw·Hill Companies

1 2 3 4 5 6 7 8 9 0   DOC/DOC   9 0 4 3 2 1 0 9

ISBN 0-07-134767-4

Printed and bound by R. R. Donnelley & Sons Company.

This book is printed on recycled, acid-free paper containing a minimum of 50% recycled de-inked fiber.

*To our wives, Melissa and Jill, for their support,
and to the traders, students, and staff who have given us
the opportunity to create this resource.*

—M.F and G.W.

To my wife Lisa, for her unwavering confidence.

—J.B.

Disclaimer

The authors and publisher assume no responsibilities for actions taken by readers. The authors and publisher are not providing investment advice. The authors and publisher do not make any claims, promises, or guarantees that any suggestions, systems, trading strategies, or information will result in a profit, loss, or any other desired result. All readers assume all risk, including but not limited to the risk of losses.

Contents

Acknowledgments

Special thanks to Jonathan Burton for all the hard work and effort he dedicated to this project, to Phyllis Davis for her speedy transcription work, and to Jeffrey Krames, who gave us the inspiration to write a second book.

—M.F. and G.W.

Heartfelt appreciation to the many day traders who bared their innermost thoughts and beliefs to a complete stranger. Without them, this book would not have been possible.

—J.B.

The New Trading Elite

Wall Street professionals have the ability to make fortunes. No, they are not geniuses nor do they possess superhuman traits. Quite simply, they maintain an edge over the rest of us. Market makers, specialists, and members of Wall Street's elite trading firms have long been able to capitalize on their monopoly for instant access to information and rapid, low-cost order executions. These advantages were available only to those who paid the high cost of exchange membership or who invested millions. The reward has been trading capabilities that are virtually simultaneous with the action on the trading floor.

Today, that same instant market access and low-cost trading are available to anyone, anywhere. Technological advancements and regulatory changes have broken Wall Street's monopoly, making it possible for individual traders and investors to participate in the market on a level playing field.

The Electronic Day Trader (McGraw-Hill, 1998), our first book, describes in detail the methods used by Wall Street professionals and how you can take advantage of today's technology to apply similar strategies. *Electronic Day Traders' Secrets* will provide you with insights from a unique group of individuals who have applied these strategies to cut substantially into the profits of Wall Street professionals.

Recently, several highly regarded Wall Street veterans have derided the business of day trading. One suggested that, in his 30-year career, he had never met a day trader who made money. Another remarked that day traders were beating the system for millions of dollars and encouraged regulators and the press to expose the "truth" of day trading.

The first remark carries some validity. Indeed, for most of the past 30 years, independent traders have been forced to use delayed quote feeds and pay exorbitant commissions, and so had little chance of making money. In addition, technology is no substitute for training. Day traders today who do not take the time to educate themselves about trading are destined to fail. Finally, the unfortunate fact is that most day traders today do lose money. But it's not that day trading is a losing proposition. For those who are persistent and resilient and take calculated risk, there is opportunity. In fact, today's day traders have unprecedented opportunity.

The second remark suggests that someone should go undercover to disclose how individuals are somehow taking advantage of the system to make millions. So we did. The result, *Electronic Day Trader's Secrets*, tells in their own words exactly how these individuals are succeeding.

Day trading has taken Wall Street by storm and is playing havoc with its long-standing, inbred traditions. Some regard day trading as the Yellow Brick Road to riches and independence. Others demonize it as an ominous gang of cyber-punks who are somehow cheating the system and profiting from the misfortune of others. But those perceptions ignore the bottom-line question: why is this phenomenon sweeping the markets?

There is one important reason. The real story is that the growth of day trading is the result of a fundamental change in the way individuals can access the stock market. In today's trading arena, individuals have the unprecedented ability to interact directly with those who set the bid and ask prices for securities. Day trading in its current form evolved not only from changes in regulations, but also from massive technological advancements. Together, these powerful twin forces have caused radical changes in the way individuals approach equity markets, and the effect has rippled through Wall Street. The uproar you hear is the sound of Wall Street being transformed into Main Street.

Regulatory Change

Industry professionals such as NASDAQ market makers or New York Stock Exchange (NYSE) specialists have long enjoyed a seemingly unbeatable edge over the individual investor. They have had better access to information, but most important, they have had better and more efficient access to the markets. They could execute their orders faster, more effectively, and for less money than the individual investor. The greatest disparities were evident in the NASDAQ market. Between 1994 and 1997, the Securities and Exchange Commission (SEC) influenced and enacted major regulatory changes that have had the most far-reaching impact on NASDAQ since its inception in 1970. They are the most significant changes to the markets since the revolutionary "May Day" in 1975, which marked the end of fixed commissions on Wall Street. These historical changes resulted in two major benefits to both individual investors and day traders: narrower spreads and fairer representation in the marketplace. Together, these add up to a dramatic reduction in the cost of buying and selling NASDAQ stocks.

The SEC, in an effort to eliminate the long-standing disparities between the ways in which individuals, professionals, and market makers accessed the NASDAQ market, forced the market makers to create more competitive markets and narrow their spreads. Market makers then, as now, were providing liquidity for public customers, but in such a manner that there was a high cost to the individual built into each transaction. This cost came in the form of a large spread between the price a customer would pay for a stock and the price that a seller was willing to accept. Wide spreads made it virtually impossible for the individual to compete.

The second aspect under scrutiny was the fact that customer limit orders—orders which have specific prices attached to their instructions for execution—were not being represented to the rest of the trading community. As a result, buyers and sellers of NASDAQ stocks were either buying from market makers or selling to market makers, as opposed to buying and selling at what should have been the best available price. This frequently resulted in market makers taking advantage of customer orders only when market conditions were in their favor. Often, market makers would engage in free-arbitrage situations where they were only filling limit buy orders when stocks were trading lower and, conversely, filling limit sell orders when stocks were trading higher. Market makers were able to take advantage of limit orders because they were not required to display customer orders in the market.

In other words, customers who would have wanted to trade with each other were not able to do so. For example, if the best displayed bid on the National Market System was at 50½ and the best displayed offer was at 51, and one customer placed an order to sell at 50¾ and another entered a buy at 50¾, the market maker who held both of the orders was not required to pair off the buyer and seller by letting them trade with each other. Instead, the market maker could wait to see which direction the stock moved. If the market maker was able to sell the stock at a price higher than 50¾, he or she would buy the stock from the customer who wanted to sell and then keep the difference between the two prices. The same would happen in reverse with the sell order. If the market maker could purchase stock lower than 50¾, he or she would sell stock to the other customer at 50¾ and again keep the difference. One market maker might even be holding 50⅞ bids, while a market maker at another firm held 50⅝ offers. Since neither quote was displayed, both orders were likely to go unexecuted.

In January 1997, the SEC changed all this when it enacted the *order handling rules,* which forced market makers to either immediately execute their customers' orders or display them in a quote that is accessible to all other participants in the marketplace. The "display rule" was a great stride toward giving customers the ability to have their orders widely distributed rather than executed only when market conditions were favorable to market makers. This is because market makers are now obligated to represent their customer limit orders in the National Market System, as opposed to holding them in-house.

A second aspect of the order handling rules was created to increase market transparency. Until January 1997 there were two markets for NASDAQ stocks: the National Market System and Instinet, an electronic communications network (ECN). The National Market System reflected the prices at which the market makers were willing to buy and sell from the public, while Instinet was generally available only to represent the interests of large institutions and select brokerage firms. In essence, there were two separate markets: one for professionals and the other for individuals. Thus, disparities in these markets were easily exploited by professionals who had access to both markets, in contrast to individuals who had access only to the quote displayed on the National Market System. The rules enacted in 1997 sought to create a single market to display the best prices available anywhere. This rule led to the proliferation of ECNs, such as Island, which allow individuals to post bids and offers along (or on parity) with market makers. ECNs make it possible for individuals to trade directly with other individuals without having to use an intermediary (market maker) to get an execution.

Technology

Today's technology has provided individuals, regardless of their location, with instant access to information. New sources are popping up daily that, in some cases, provide not just instant information, but also instant executions. From their own homes or offices, individuals can gain access to the same information previously available only to professionals. Two important factors are NASDAQ Level 2 quotes and direct-access executions.

Following is a simplified Level 2 quote for Yahoo (YHOO):

YHOO	50¾	X	51
	10 GSCO		3 SBSH
	20 MLCO		7 ISLD

The first part of this quote reads as follows: The best bid in YHOO is currently 50¾ and the best offer is 51. NASDAQ refers to this part of the quote as its *Level 1* quote, which is widely available through most brokerage firms. Below this quote is some additional information: Goldman Sachs (GSCO) and Merrill Lynch (MLCO) are willing to pay 15¾ for 1000 (or 10 round lots of 100 shares) and 2000 shares, respectively. The best offer in the stock is 51. Smith Barney (SBSH) and the Island ECN (ISLD) are willing to sell 300 and 700 shares, respectively. This additional information constitutes the NASDAQ *Level 2* quote. A Level 2 quote lists all of the current market participants, along with how much they would like to trade and at what price. This additional information is also easily accessible to anyone through various online brokerages.

The proliferation of ECNs has played a significant role in allowing individual investors to avoid the heavy tolls of market-maker spreads, enabling them to represent their orders in an efficient manner and on parity with Wall Street market makers.

Note that in the preceding quote, ISLD is on the offer, which is likely an order entered by a customer directly into the market. This offer is displayed in the same fashion as that of any large institution or market maker and has essentially become part of the quote. Also note that this trader is attempting to sell stock on the offer side of the spread rather than selling it to a market maker on the bid (GSCO or MLCO), as an investor would have had to do in the past. Previously, a trader would have given the same order to the broker, who had much more freedom and flexibility in whether to execute it. Day traders now have the ability to "save the spread"—sell on the offer rather than at the lower-price bid.

Direct-Access Executions

Electronic day trading has been embraced by a wide variety of investors and traders and is being carried out through various systems. In the past few years, millions of investors and traders of all types have opened accounts to access the market via the Internet. Brokerage firms of all sizes have attempted to capitalize on this trend. In general, most electronic traders stand to benefit from lower commissions, faster executions, and better access to information, as opposed to those who use a traditional broker. For the professional day trader, four factors matter most: speed, reliability, information (NASDAQ Level 2), and direct-access executions.

The most important distinction between the typical Internet system and online systems preferred by day traders such as those you will read about in this book is the way in which the orders are actually routed for execution. Most online systems route their customer order flow to a third party, who then pays them for the right to trade the orders. This third party is generally a market-maker firm that is attempting to capitalize on earning the spread. If the stock is not immediately executable, the market maker is supposed to represent the order in the market in a reasonable amount of time. Unfortunately, what is reasonable to one may not be to another. In fact, any time delay is critical to the day trader. Yet payment for order flow in this manner is a fairly common industry practice. Many of the largest online firms do not like to advertise that they participate in these relationships, for if a third party is willing to pay for the right to execute a customer order, it's because they believe there's a profit to be made. As a result, in some cases, a customer may not be receiving the best possible execution.

In contrast, high-end online systems used by day traders not only feature Level 2 quotes, but allow individuals to place their own orders directly into the marketplace through the use of an ECN or order-entry system. These systems give traders the ability to send orders electronically to the NYSE specialist via Designated Order Turnaround (DOT), as well as effectively use NASDAQ's execution systems or represent their limit orders using ECNs. This way, the investor knows exactly where an order is going and how it is being represented. These systems are also designed to deliver what often seem like instant executions.

While the average online customer may make two or three trades a month, it would not be uncommon for the day traders described in this book to make upward of one, two, or even three hundred trades per day. Several brokerages offer the high-end systems that cater to professional day traders. While small in number compared to the whole of online accounts, these traders can generate a significant amount of trading volume. The combination of millions of online accounts and the volume generated by what is estimated to be several thousand professional day traders may represent 20 to 30 percent of the average daily volumes of the NYSE and NASDAQ. This number is rapidly growing as more investors shed their traditional relationships with stockbrokers to take advantage of online trading and investing. All stand to benefit in numerous ways, and the pages that follow feature interviews with traders who have made lucrative careers by capitalizing on these changes.

Realistic Expectations

Today's day traders hail from diverse backgrounds and professions. Lawyers, doctors, brokers, market makers, college graduates, college dropouts, and many others have left the mainstream to pursue what could be one of the most exciting and rewarding careers for the twenty-first century. Recent market volatility and speculation in new Internet-related companies such as Yahoo! and Amazon.com have further fueled the excitement surrounding day trading. This volatility has allowed some of the best day traders to make more money than they ever thought possible. Top day traders can make millions of dollars a year trading with their own money for their own accounts.

The media have picked up on the amazing earning potential of day traders. Twenty-something whiz kids have been featured in prominent publications such as *Forbes*, *The New York Times*, and *Newsweek*. Traders and founders of day-trading brokerages are frequently interviewed on financial television shows on CNN and CNBC. A fair amount of this media attention has focused on some of the individuals interviewed in this book.

Unfortunately, this glossy media image does not quite reflect the reality. Some traders have been extremely successful—but don't quit your day job just yet. The idea of quitting your job and making more money in a day than most make in a year by trading stocks sounds tempting, but it's too good to be true. The rule changes have made it possible for individuals to participate more fairly in the markets, but they are up against market makers and other professionals who have consistently made money in those markets and are good at what they do. Market makers are well-trained and well-capitalized traders. You will need to be in the same league before you can compete against them.

The traders interviewed in this book generally started with between $50,000 and $150,000 in capital. Most suffered substantial losses at first, but all turned the corner within their first year and went on to great success. They are survivors, but they learned the hard way that day trading is not for everyone, and money and stamina are no guarantees.

It's said that the easiest way to succeed is to find someone who is getting the results you want and copy them. This book opens that window to some of the best day traders now in the business.

Andrew Friis
Looks Can Be Deceiving

"Any number of traders can enter a good trade. The best traders know how to exit, but not out of necessity. Great traders sell when they can, not when they have to."

If there's a cure for trader's slump, Andrew Friis would probably discover it. He studied to be a doctor, after all, training his analytical mind on an undergraduate premed program that eventually would have led him into private practice.

Friis was looking for a high-pressure career, a way to be deep in the action. In his third year of college, he decided that medicine wasn't going to satisfy him in that way. A friend had moved to New York and landed a job trading on the floor of the American Stock Exchange. The high speed of the chase appealed to Friis, and the first time he walked onto the Exchange floor, he was hooked.

That was in 1994, when Friis was just 22. He cut his teeth in the equity options pit, and a couple of years later, when the opportunity arose to day trade his own account, Friis was ready. He scraped together enough working capital, took a seat in front of a computer, and started watching the activity on the screen.

Now 27, Friis has moved his practice to the calmer climes of Boca Raton, Florida. But don't equate the tranquility of South Florida with Friis's competitive, hurricane-like trading. And in the way a doctor would carry a black bag of medical tools, Friis keeps a full kit of mental tools tucked inside a storehouse of experience.

One useful device he employs is akin to a simple stethoscope, able to filter out the market's noise and listen to its inner beat. It's not skepticism, which only sours people on their task. It's a powerful insight, through which a trader realizes that things are not always what they seem. As Friis puts it, looks can be deceiving. That understanding alone brings greater mobility and flexibility to a trader's game. With this recognition, you're better able to dodge the obstacles that can wreck rival traders, and to recognize those opportunities they miss.

■   ■   ■

Your initiation to trading came on the rough-and-tumble floor of the American Stock Exchange, which at first must have seemed like you'd landed on another planet. You wanted action, and you found it. What's the Exchange like?

The floor of a stock exchange is a wild place—if you don't know what's going on. If you do, then everything that you see and hear means something. If you can block out the useless information and are able to focus on what's important, then you're ahead of those traders around you who are caught up in less-important events. You have to use tunnel vision, much like any elite athlete does. A good hitter supposedly can count the stitches on a fastball. That's the zone you have to put your-self in.

How do you get into this "zone"? Is this ability something innate or is it acquired over time?

It's both. If you don't have innate concentration abilities and are easily distracted, you're not necessarily going to make a good trader. On the trading floor, you block out everything that's going on around you and focus on your business. Then you have a higher chance of success. It took me a while to get acclimated. Once I was, it became a place to thrive.

What kind of business did you have at the Exchange?

Trading options. I started out as an order clerk and then traded options on the floor.

What did you learn at the Exchange that has helped you as an electronic day trader?

Looks can be deceiving. When things look their worst, often there is a silver lining. When the crowd mentality is at its fury point and people are at the point of fracture, usually that presents the best opportunities. *When everyone is on one side of the market, it doesn't mean that everyone is right.*

It's interesting that you say that looks can be deceiving, because you alluded to the same perception when you talked about the stock exchange. To an outside observer, the floor of an exchange seems chaotic. People are scream-ing and waving their hands. But there is a method to the madness; traders are following an orderly, accepted process. With electronic day trading, though, you don't

have that physical ability to see through the bluster. All you have is a flickering screen.

You can tell, by watching the particular market makers and the pricing action of the stock, when the right time is to get in and to get out. The pricing action in electronic day trading comes to a crescendo at a point where the buying and selling action has leveled off; that is usually the best point to enter or exit a trade.

Finding that point is what takes experience and is what makes good traders. It's very hard to teach textbook electronic day trading. You don't have a crowd mentality; you don't have the decibel level and the furied action to look at. All you have is your own sense of when the buying and selling equals out. *When stocks are moving, there is always a greater number of buyers or a greater number of sellers. At a certain point that will balance out. That is when the most high-probability or high-percentage trades are entered or exited.*

So although day trading doesn't give you a crowd to watch, you do find clues in share volume.

Share volume and market-maker movement. The degree of market-maker movement will tell you whether orders are thinning out or are still heavy. That's where you will find the entrance and exit points.

You're describing a sweet spot, a point where you're going to get a hit. What sort of stocks do you like to bat with?

High-volume, high-price-movement NASDAQ stocks. Most day traders are looking for action. A big price movement intraday, corresponding with good volume, that's where you will find me and other day traders. I've been trading the same group of technology stocks—semiconductors, box makers, computer-chip makers, networking—like Intel and Cisco Systems. That's where you are going to find the biggest gainers and share volume.

Other traders don't necessarily trade those high-volume highflyers. They'll try to find their own niche, take advantage of spreads, and become their own market maker. My game is to find stocks with a nice range today and try to buy when they've dipped and sell when they trade higher. And don't fight the market trend during the day. I'm buying strong stocks on the dips and selling them on upswings, so I'm always on the right side of the market.

What if you have an opinion about a stock? That's a good way to wind up on the wrong side of the trade.

I take educated opinions. If the market seems to be turning higher, I won't short. I buy strong stocks that are up on the day. I don't buy stocks that are down on the day if the market is going up. I don't sell short upstocks on an up day. I sell stocks short that are negative. It's simple supply and demand. I'm not Goldman Sachs or Morgan Stanley. I'm just trying to find the action. I want to follow the big guys. If a stock is up on the day, it means there are a lot more buyers than sellers. I would never try to be a seller. I would only be a buyer, and vice versa with the short side.

Subjective decisions have no place in your game.

I'm just a trader. I'm not trying to fight the powers of economic balance. All I trade off is my own thinking, my own mind, and I'm not any smarter than the other guy. The day I lose the most amount of money is when the situation or reason for entering a trade changes and I'm too stubborn or too slow to see that and shift my position. *Successful traders are able to perceive a bad trade and get out. If you're able to do that in a timely manner, then you're putting yourself ahead of guys who don't really know a bad trade until after it happens.*

A bad trade forces you to accept that you blew it. You're going to be out money; the question is how much.

Controlling losses and getting out of trades is a lot harder than entering trades. *Any number of traders can enter a good trade. The best traders know how to exit, but not out of necessity. Great traders sell when they can, not when they have to.*

There's a fine line between stubbornness and having courage of conviction.

That's the fundamental difference between a good trader and a bad trader—someone who gets involved in the trade because it was the right trade to make, not because he's made or lost money. The monetary aspect shouldn't really enter here. The trade might still be good even though you are down. You might just have entered or exited at the incorrect time.

How much are you willing to let a trade go against you before getting nervous?

If I enter a trade for a reason, and that reason doesn't change, then I don't exit the trade even if it's against me. All you're trying to do is increase your winning percentage by keeping cool and taking advantage of people who are not.

Can you relate a situation where your conviction carried through?

The semiconductor group has been in a downturn, and the bellwether semiconductor stock, Intel, has been acting poorly. But the market today was strong. So I shorted Intel.

But you've just said that the market is up, and presumably Intel is riding along with it.

Given the rule I mentioned about selling short in an upmarket, why would I enter that trade? Because Intel has been weak. The whole semiconductor group, as I said, has been very weak. So although the market is going higher, my reason for shorting Intel is that it's a weak stock in a weak group. When the market does trade lower, Intel should fall much faster than the market. The market now is on the opposite side of my trade, but as long as the stocks in the sector don't lose their weak status, I'm going to hold my short in Intel.

How did this Intel trade conclude?

It played out well. The market was strong, but the semiconductor group was weak. When the market started to turn, Intel, as predicted, was the first stock to fall—and it fell quite a bit. I made a point and a half on that trade.

A key to the success of this trade is that you had a good working knowledge of the stock and its industry. You had seen where Intel was coming from.

I knew where Intel was coming from; I had watched it for a couple of days. I knew it was weak and that there were still sellers out there. I knew that if I did put a short on and the market turned in my favor—down a bit—then Intel should be the first stock to fall.

That's fine logic for entering a trade. How did you know when to get out?

Well, my reason never changed, so I'm still in the trade.

You took a profitable short position home overnight?

Yes, I'm short Intel overnight. As I said, my reason never changed. The group got weaker, and the market got weaker. Until that changes, I'm going to hold onto the short until I see that the market environment or the trading environment has changed.

What will shake you out? If Intel gaps down at the open, wouldn't you close the gate and move on?

Trading gaps are different. If the stock gaps down $1 tomorrow, I'll take my profit and that will be the end of the trade. In that situation, I would never look a gift horse in the mouth. You might say that is the opposite of what I just said about the market changing. But the market situation did change. The stock didn't just trade down, it actually gapped down $1. From that situation, I'm given a handsome profit.

So to your way of thinking, a change in the market doesn't necessarily require a tectonic shift of investor sentiment. A gap down is enough; you're basically being handed money.

If you make a good trade, you have to take a profit. No one has ever gone poor taking profits. If you made the trade for a reason, and now they just tripled your money on the opening of the market, then take that profit.

Some traders prefer to avoid stocks that are about to announce earnings. The market is merciless to companies

that miss analysts' estimates of quarterly income figures. Anyone on the wrong side of the trade can get hammered. Do you steer clear of stocks when they're about to release earnings?

I will avoid holding a stock into earnings. But just before the earnings come out, I would just trade it like any other. If it's screaming up, then I would look for a good place to enter and buy. If it was getting sold off, then I would find a good place to enter a sale. I wouldn't sell frivolously or buy out of pure greed or lust for the stock.

You bring up an important point—approaching a trade analytically and logically, without trying to cut corners. You've said that you look for action, but it's notable how different people play the same scene. Some get into a frenetic, knee-jerk mind-set. Others just follow the book.

If you're able to make rational decisions under pressure, those are usually the most profitable trades. But you can't just trade off instinct, and you can't just trade off discipline—you have to have a bit of both.

Describe the pressure of a trade. Does the strain come from the money you can make and lose, or is it something less tangible?

It's the feeling of being squeezed, of not really knowing where you are. A lot of times you are in a trade and it doesn't go your way, and you get a feeling of being lost. That's uncomfortable. This is a game of using your brain to analyze your way through a maze like the stock market. If you get lost, pressure builds. *Getting lost in a trade usually means that you're not on the right side.* You panic. In your mind, the ways you were trained to get out of trades come to a standstill. You don't know which direction to take. *It's hard for traders under pressure to make decisions based on rational thought, not fear.*

Any anxious and lost trader is looking for an exit strategy. There aren't too many choices. You either land safely or bail out.

If you're smart and are in this game for the long haul, you'll learn from the decision. If you exit the trade at a loss, watch the price action afterward and figure out what you did wrong. I see all day long where I went wrong, and I try to correct that by not falling into the same traps.

Lost in a trade, you're on your own. There are no friendly natives around to give directions. How do you create an escape route?

I take a mental step back and evaluate the overall picture before I make a decision. If the overall picture hasn't changed, the reason for entering a trade hasn't changed, I will stop myself from making that decision in haste. I want to cut the rope, to stop the bleeding, but again, if I take a step back and don't lose my cool, then I'm able to make a decision based on rational thought.

You're talking now about having discipline. That's an important attribute of winning traders, and one of the crucial rules of the game. Can you recall a point in your trading where discipline helped you advance from being a break-even or average trader to a more consistent winner?

I started in an office with a group of traders, and I started to make a few dollars. Then one trader started making a lot more money than any of us, consistently. At that point I made the decision that I needed to make more money than that guy.

You "needed" to make more money? It became competitive.

I was making $1500 a day, and then I saw this guy across the room making $5000 a day. I moved myself next to him. I asked the office manager if I could move and he said, "Why would you move? You're making $1500 a day; you're doing great." I told him that while I might be making $1500, the guy two seats over to the right is making $5000, and I want to find out what he is doing right.

Now $1500 profit—if you multiply that over about 240 trading days a year—is roughly $360,000 before taxes. Someone pulling down five grand a day is going home with $1.2 million. So for obvious reasons, you move closer. What happened next?

I fed off of him. *Day trading is a learning experience, and you can never learn enough. I learn every day, no matter how much money I'm making.* If this particular trader is doing better than I am, then I want to find out what he's doing. Whether it's the stocks he's trading or how he's entering and exiting his trades, I want to watch what he's doing right that I'm not. There is no such thing as a perfect trader. But if you can increase your percentage of profitable trades, then you can only increase your profitability.

What skill did he have that was eluding you?

I wasn't timing the trades as well as he was. I might have been making ¼ of a point, but this guy might be making ⅜ because he was in a drop faster than me.

Your timing wasn't as good. But you were clearing $1500 a day. Pretty soon you're talking about real money.

If I'm making trades that are 50 percent accurate and there are traders who are 60 percent accurate, the monetary issue doesn't come into play. You could do the math and figure out how much money you're making, but for me it's not necessarily a game of money—it's a game of success and of winning. If I'm able to increase my percentage of profitable trades by watching this trader—focus more, buy stocks with more decisiveness, and increase those winning percentage trades—then I'm able to increase my own take. Watching him, I learned that this game is a lot more focused and concentrated than I had thought. And I honed my skills.

Now you had better ability, but did you have a better income?

I started making $3000 or $4000 in a day—but he was making $5000. And I said, "I don't care if it's $5 or $5 million, I have to make more than he does." The competition aspect came out, and that's important to traders as well. *Complacency causes a lot of traders to start losing money. Whenever you feel happy with your results, then you're prone to get knocked off your pedestal.*

Did you finally reach a point where you could claim victory over this rival trader?

I was making a little more money than him, but instead of me listening to him, he was trying to follow the trades I was doing. I wasn't feeding off his information; he was feeding off mine. That's when I knew I had beaten him.

Randy Guttenberg
Anticipate Change

"If my head is not 100 percent into it, I'm not trading at peak performance. It's better just to go home. Focus and concentration are critical."

Experienced day traders often speak of a powerful gut feeling that guides them through the market's twists and turns. And though they find this emotion difficult to describe, some credit is due to diligent hard work, whether you're a day trader or a day laborer, that ultimately develops strong confidence and skilled competence.

What is the essence of this gut feeling? For Randy Guttenberg, a 28-year-old New York–based day trader, it's the ability to anticipate change in market action and then respond in a realistic fashion. That means not panicking when a trade goes against you, and staying cool when you're raking in profits. It means knowing a stock's levels—its bid and ask history since that morning's opening bell—so that you can properly gauge the direction of its next move. And it requires the mental gymnastics of separating the day's strong stocks from the weak so you know which stocks to buy and which to sell short.

Put another way, you have to follow the money flow. Trouble is, every other trader with a modem and a hard drive has the same goal. Guttenberg's strength is his ability to make split-second, *reasoned* decisions. That's crucial. The key is to be better than your rivals not only in speed but, more important, in common sense. By anticipating change, you minimize surprises. By reacting with reason and not emotion, you're able to roll with the punches—and throw a few as well.

■   ■   ■

Day trading involves quite a few hard-and-fast rules, which traders prioritize to best fit their personality and style. What is your top trading rule?

Discipline. If I'm wrong, I have no problem taking my loss. If I'm right and I'm comfortable in the position, I'll hold on and try to let my winners run. Discipline is cutting losses, and also being patient with respect to getting the best price. I don't jump just because I see a stock in motion. Instead, I try to bid for the strong stocks on pullbacks so that I get a good price. It gives me added confidence, which allows me to hold onto the stock a little longer and take a larger profit out. A lot of people are afraid of missing a move. But if you miss it, you miss it. Then you've got to reassess the situation and the price and get back in at appropriate levels.

Why not jump aboard a moving train? Grabbing that momentum seems like a sure ticket.

Because sometimes you get on at the end of the line. Maybe the stock's already moved a half or $1. It's better to get in on pullbacks than to chase a stock and bid it up. You end up buying stock from people who bought into the move earlier.

Knowing where the stock is coming from gives you perspective. You know what you're getting relative to the potential move. Certain stocks act in predictable ways, like Dell Computer. If Dell makes a move, I would expect a half to maybe $1. If I get into Dell after it's already moved, it becomes a lower-probability trade because I've already missed a good portion of the run.

How can you work a trade to your advantage so that you minimize any nasty surprises?

Have a game plan. When I first started, I didn't have a strategy. I would see a big move in the Standard & Poor's 500 stock index futures and I'd want to buy some stock. So I would think, what should I buy? But the futures had already started to make their move. I wasn't getting in early enough. I would pay up for stocks and wasn't capitalizing on them.

Now I keep a list of stocks that I feel are strong and acting well relative to the market. I also make a list of stocks that I feel are weak. This way, if I see a major move in the S&P futures, I can act immediately. I don't have to start asking what's strong and what's not. A game plan helps me get into positions better because I have anticipated the move by watching stocks all day. If it's a strong stock, I'll buy it. So if the futures are strong and, for instance, I've identified Dell as a strong stock, I would bid for Dell on a pullback, hoping it will rally along with the market. If I'm wrong, I can probably get out within ⅛ or so of my purchase price. If I'm right, I'm early enough that I can let it run a half point or better.

How many stocks do you follow?

On a daily basis I probably look at 10 to 15 stocks, but I concentrate on the big-name technology stocks and the Internet stocks because they do have wide ranges and large price swings. The Internet stocks also tend to have wider bid and ask spreads. I take more risk in stocks like Amazon.com or Yahoo!, so I should get more out of the trade. Whereas many of these big-name tech stocks like Dell or Cisco Systems have more market makers and narrow spreads. You can get out easily, so there's not as much risk there.

The computer screen is your window on the trading world. When you stare at it, you're searching for clues and answers. But what are the basic questions you're asking?

How many market makers are at each level? How many market makers are at the current bid and the current offer? What is the next price, and how many market makers are at that level? If I see five market makers bidding $100, and five below them bidding $99⅞, then I can make a good assumption of how I would be able to get out and at what price.

One day, for example, the market was up but Dell was not acting well. Every time the S&P futures started to rally, Dell was not going as far as expected. So when the futures started to come in, Dell was on my list as a potential short. If it wasn't that strong when the market was rallying, we could see a greater pullback if the market started to come in. I got short and the stock wiggled and jiggled, but I tried to hold on because there were so many market makers at each level. Even if five of them lifted, I'm only risking another ⅛ or so. I was able to hold on and made a point and a half on the trade. But sometimes these stocks move so quickly that if you can't get out at a good price, they move against you just as fast.

It also helps when you can identify a market maker who is potentially the last person on the bid or holds the bid for an extended period. Say the market looks like it's going to continue downward and Morgan Stanley, for example, is the only guy on the bid, just taking on stock. Maybe he's got a buy order, maybe he's the buyer. You never know. We don't have the order flow; we don't actually see what they're doing. We just try to read the tape.

Suppose you do get shaken out, and then the stock takes off. Do you immediately jump in?

I would get back in. But I'd want to watch it first to get a better feel for what's going on. I like to be comfortable in the stocks I'm trading. So if I've watched them myself and have a good idea of the range of the pullbacks and the upside, then I can hold on a lot better. Again, a lot of it is simply getting in at the right price. If you have a tendency to buy a stock at the high end of the range, then there's more panic. But if I get in at a good price, it allows me to hold through the wiggles and jiggles. Then I'm not really taking a loss in the stock, I just don't have the profit I did.

Many traders, anxiously watching a position go against them, might be inclined to panic.

I have panicked in the past, and I have hit the stock out at the bottom. It bothers me. Not panicking is a big factor. Everyone panics once in a while. But I try not to get emotional about the trade. When I first started trading, I was concerned about losing money. Now I say, "Okay, the stock is going down but I know it's strong. Let me buy more at a better price." That's one of the biggest differences in my trading. If the market is holding and the stock is not really going tremendously far against me, then I will look at it as a buying opportunity.

Volatility is a trader's best friend. How do you handle a stock that doesn't move, but just sits in a narrow box and refuses to budge?

In the past when my stocks weren't moving, I would get impatient and offer them out, and right after somebody bought from me it would go higher. Now, if the stock isn't doing anything—caught in a tight range—I usually do nothing. I just hold my position and wait for it to make a real move, then look to get out. If it starts to break to the downside, I'll get out immediately and limit my loss. If it breaks to the upside, I look to see how far it moves and how far it comes in on pullbacks. If the stock continues to make higher highs and higher lows, then I try to get more out of the trade because it seems to be breaking out of its range. I always keep in mind how much I'm willing to risk in relation to where I think the stock will go.

The focus and forward thinking you've been discussing neatly describe another cardinal rule of trading: anticipate changes in market conditions. How have you developed this ability?

By constantly reevaluating positions, their prices, and the strength of both the stock and the market. A lot of it involves seeing a stock not acting as it should in relation to the S&P 500 futures. If the futures go higher and my stock that I thought was really strong can't follow, then I start to think maybe the buyers are done and there's a change in the overall trend of the stock. The time of day also influences my opinion. If a strong stock pulls in during the middle of the day, I don't look at that as necessarily a change in the overall trend, but maybe more that the market makers are knocking it down to buy some stock back at a better price. But if it's 3:30 P.M. and the futures are going higher and the stock is selling off, then I might think the trend has changed. The futures are moving up—how come my stock isn't acting like it should?

The same is true when the futures are dropping. The other day I was trading Cisco Systems and the S&P futures fell 11 points. So I shorted Cisco because it looked weak. But Cisco didn't go down at all. If the futures are down 11 points—which is significant—you would tend to think that a weak stock also would move lower. So as soon as the futures started to turn higher, I covered my short and got long. I bought 8000 shares. Here was a weak stock that didn't go down with the market. So everyone else who thought it was going down is not only going to have to cover their shorts, but someone like me who had identified a change in the trend in the stock will be looking to get long.

The stock ran about a dollar. Cisco was my best trade of that day. I was anticipating not only a move in the stock but what everyone else was going to do in reaction. But you really need to be on top of your game. *You need to be 150 percent focused on what's going on in the market so that you can react quickly*—in this case, over 5 or 10 minutes.

Day trading is obviously an "of the moment" experience— no one knows what will happen with a stock between the opening and closing bells. But this insta-trading also involves some predetermined expectations about stocks, like gauging relative strength and weakness. Can this measure really help to predict a stock's direction?

If a stock has been trading strong, I would expect that to continue unless there are major changes in the market or in the way the stock is acting. The other day, for example, there was news that Peapod (PPOD) is in a marketing deal with Excite, one of the larger Internet players. I thought it could be good news for PPOD, so I was keeping my eye on the stock. It was acting well, and though it wasn't doing much around midday, I felt that a reaction might come later.

About 3:15 P.M.—45 minutes before the close—I saw market makers bidding up the stock. A lot of times stocks tend to have a real move in the morning, jiggle around during the middle of the day, and then have more real moves at the end of the day. I saw the activity pick up in PPOD and watched it move higher. It started to pull in a little, and I found a price where it seemed to have settled and didn't look like it was going lower. So I took the offer and it started to make its way higher. I got in after it had made an initial move, but I still made about ⅝ on the trade.

Pocketing ⅝ of a point on 1000 shares is clearly a win; that's a fast 625 bucks. But this particular trade sounds risky on two counts: taking stock at the offer and getting in after its upside breakout.

I was watching the way it was acting and it just wasn't selling off. Market makers were moving from the offer side to the bid side. There were more people trying to buy the stock than trying to get out. I was bidding myself and nobody would sell to me. And the price began to climb. I thought then that the only way I would be able to get in was to take the offer.

So you had a certain comfort level with the trade because you could determine the liquidity and could feel a floor underneath.

It helps to know the risk/reward trade-off for the level that I'm buying at. On stocks that have wider spreads and fewer market makers at each level, I know I'm risking a little more if

I'm unable to get out for the best bid price. But I also know where the next bid is below that. And if I see a market maker who is constantly on the bid even as the stock is going down, I might hold on longer, knowing that he's a buyer and is holding that price. I don't have to panic out of the trade, because I've got buyers on my side.

Panic surely must be the undoing of many traders, especially those who brashly barge on the scene ready to land the big prize. What's the secret to longevity in this game?

Being able to control your losses and to let your profits run. Experience counts. *You find yourself in the same situations many times, so a lot of it is just a matter of learning to do the right thing.* Not long ago, for instance, AMAT—Applied Materials—came out with good earnings and opened maybe $7 higher. I thought there might be a sell-off since the stock had opened up so much. I got short the stock—and it wouldn't go down. Not a tick. The market makers obviously had a lot of buy orders and there was no sell-off at all. Now if a stock can't go down when the market pulls in, then you would expect that stock to rally when the market does. So I was able to cover my short and maybe I lost ⅛ on the trade, but I wasn't able to get into it long because I didn't react quickly enough. So I didn't have a long position in the stock as it began to go higher.

That lost opportunity must have stayed front and center with you.

It did. About a week later, Dell reports earnings and opens up about $8 or $9. I thought there might be a sell-off, although I'm remembering AMAT. Nevertheless, I got short Dell. Then the stock looked like it was holding—just like AMAT did—so I covered my short immediately at even money and went long. This time, when the stock began to run I was able to capitalize on the trade. You learn from mistakes so that you can react positively the next time.

Is it safe to assume that, like most beginning traders, you lost money early on?

A lot of money. I didn't know how to get into trades at the right places. I didn't want to lose money, and that probably caused me to lose more.

How did the fear of losing lead to greater losses?

Scared money never wins. The S&P futures would make these big moves, and I was leery. Then all of a sudden the stocks that I wanted to buy had started moving. So I would see the momentum and buy it, but I hadn't anticipated the move. If anything, I was getting in at the top, buying from people who were looking to sell—like day traders taking their profits. They had gotten in a half point earlier than me, and now the stock was going down.

Here I was trying to learn and didn't want to lose any money, so I would sell it out and lose ⅛. I had to work on getting my timing down and getting in at better prices. As time went on, I had more winning trades and felt more confident. I was able to anticipate more.

What was the turning point?

It helped when I learned to become more patient and more calm, to control my emotions and be more confident about what I thought was going to happen. A lot of times I was correct in my assumptions, but I wasn't reacting properly. And there were times when I would try to limit my losses and get out of a trade that was a good trade, but I was letting emotions take over. I was aggravated and disappointed in myself because I had been good at other things in the past and I was unsatisfied with my trading. I would see other people doing well and thought there was no reason that I couldn't do just as well.

Trading does leave plenty of room for self-doubt.

In the beginning, there is a lot of second-guessing. Then I learned to take things slower. *It's said that 80 percent of trading is mental—how you're feeling, your psyche.* If you have a bad day at home or you don't sleep that night, maybe then you come in and don't have a good trading day because you're not concentrating and you're not focused.

So winning trades are due largely to the power of positive thinking?

If my head is not 100 percent into it, I'm not trading at peak performance. It's better just to go home. Focus and concentration are critical.

I'm successful when I'm concentrating and know exactly what's going on. When I'm not doing well, one thing that helps me out of my rut is I get smaller and take one trade at a time. I try to get the pendulum back in my direction, looking to make just one winning trade. When you get frustrated, you need to take a step back. Maybe I'll go for a walk just to clear my head. I calm down, regroup, and get back into the battle. I trade smaller positions, and I take my profits. Then I'm not losing money anymore, I'm making it.

How does your trading style change when you're doing well?

I press it more when things are going my way. It's like in the casino—when you are up a lot of money, you are really playing with the house's money. You can be more aggressive. I might hold positions a little longer and give them more room since things are working for me.

Is day trading a casino?

It's as dangerous as one, but I wouldn't say it's a casino. We try to take educated positions in high-probability situations. Say, for example, that I'm watching Dell. I've identified that Morgan Stanley is a buyer and the stock moves up $1. The S&P futures sell off a little bit. Dell pulls in half a point, and I see Morgan Stanley is on the bid again. I know that during the day he had been holding the bid. I decide that this is a good price, and in fact every time it comes down to this price it holds. So I put out my bid and try to buy it at that price. As the futures start to tick back up, that trade would be something I would expect would work out. I would consider that a lower-risk play. In a casino, you're just rolling the dice every time.

Serge Milman
Control Losses

"Flexibility is a key to successful day trading."

He's there on the cover of *Forbes,* with an ear-to-ear grin that makes electronic day trading appear like a shortcut from Wall Street to Easy Street. It's not, as Serge Milman will be the first to admit. He'll tell you without prompting that day trading is tough, painful, competitive. He just makes it look simple.

Milman came to the United States from Russia with his family at the age of five. He grew up in Queens, New York, among hardworking immigrants, and studied computers and finance in college. Now 26, Milman has merged each of these qualities—hard work, computers, finance—into a lucrative and satisfying career. He arrives at the office more than an hour before the market opens to catch up on news and to get a sense of where the trading day might lead. At the opening bell, *he'll have an initial game plan mapped out,* but over the next 6½ hours Milman will change direction so often that his trading can seem a blur of activity. *Flexibility, in fact, is one of his keys to success as a trader,* and coupled with speed and a quick mind, enables him to capture that extra fraction of profit and keep his losses to a minimum.

These skills would be an asset to any Wall Street trading desk, but Goldman Sachs, Morgan Stanley, and Salomon Brothers didn't see that potential in Milman when he went looking for a trader's position after graduating from college in 1995. Instead he became a computer programmer for the Federal Reserve Bank of New York, making $32,000 a year and being constantly frustrated with the organizational bureaucracy. When a friend's day-trading firm needed someone to fix computers and be a clerk, Milman jumped at the chance. In August 1996, after six months of watching successful traders, he pooled enough capital and began to trade his own account.

■   ■   ■

What first led you to believe that you had a knack for trading stocks?

I found out about trading in my freshman year of college. Some of my friends who were older than me got jobs as traders or were working in trading firms. I found out about the business and what successful guys were making. And what they were doing—buying, selling—I knew that it would be for me. I've always been competitive. I've played a lot of sports. I'm not a big guy, but I'm a pretty good athlete. I think I'm bright. I'm flexible. I don't really hold opinions. Something like this—cutting-edge, fast, trading against other people—I felt that I would be pretty good at.

Where did you get the start-up capital?

I had about $15,000 in savings. I borrowed from my parents, from their friends, from my friends. If I had blown through all of my own money—the risk capital—then I would have been scared. And I did. I lost $12,000 within my first three months.

Losing so much, so quickly, can really shake you up.

And I was very conservative, humble, and modest. I was trading really small. I still lost $12,000. It seemed like a lot of money at the time. It is a lot of money. But I kept doing it and, fortunately, things turned out the way they did.

What gave you the courage to continue?

Because I knew what I was doing wrong. I just couldn't correct it. I kept a diary for six months. I used to write things like "know your levels better," "you're buying tops," "you're selling bottoms," "you're buying when you should be selling," "you're selling when you should be buying on the bid." I was doing everything wrong. I had the right ideas, but my timing was wrong. It took me a while to get my timing down, and there's nothing like good timing to build your confidence.

It seems logical that confidence would play a big role in successful day trading. What strength does it bring to the table?

If you're not confident, you're going to trade defensively. It's like driving with your foot on the brake. You're not going to trade aggressively; you're just going to go with the flow of traffic. When you're trading aggressively and with confidence, you can try to hit that home run and succeed. You can try to build a position and nail a big trade—8000 shares for a point; 9000 shares for a point and a half.

Traders often speak of their job in athletic terms like "hits" and "home runs." Every day is game day—you get pumped and take the field. Do you have a particular ritual or mind-set that you practice each morning?

I just try to relax. I come in by 8:15 A.M. I see where the Standard & Poor's 500 stock index futures are trading and how the foreign markets closed the day before. By 9:20 A.M. I have a game plan. I like to have an idea of whether I'm buying, selling, or trading the market stocks.

Does your game plan change throughout the day?

Yes. If it looks like it's going to be a particularly aggressive day, I'll start trading at the open. If it's slow, I'll wait a couple of minutes. Maybe I'm thinking about selling a stock short. I'll see what the traders next to me are doing. If I'm wrong, they don't let me forget it. It's not a short; it's a buy. So I buy. Later it becomes a short—then I'm wrong again. So I short. It's a seesaw. You try to nail that big move, but it's hard.

One reason it's hard is because so many good competitors trade just as aggressively and intelligently. Whether you trade 100 shares or 10,000 shares, you're always playing at the expert table.

The best market makers, the best traders, are on these stocks. Morgan Stanley is not going to put a rookie trader as the Dell Computer market maker. Their top two or three traders are on Dell. It's the same with Microsoft, Yahoo!, Amazon.com. These are the stocks that I trade; these are the stocks that other guys trade. And we're all looking to make that money. I've never said this is easy and I never will. Just because our hours aren't bad doesn't mean this is an easy living.

Is any of this game plan mapped out before you get to work?

No. Before I come to the office, I have no opinion of where the market is going. You have to be flexible. Flexibility is the key to successful day trading. You shouldn't come in thinking that since you've been a successful investor, you can make it as a trader. This is a completely different game. We don't care about the fundamentals. I'm not a fund manager. I'm not here to see where Dell or Intel is going to be six months or two years from now. I'm only here to trade it today. If today it looks strong, I'm looking to buy. If it looks weak, I'm looking to short—despite how good some analysts say it is. I'm just trying to play the momentum. Day trading is all about momentum and volatility. I'm always looking for news to trade. Stock splits are great; earnings reports are good; upgrades, downgrades—anything that can make the stock move up or down is something I'm looking to capture. Because when it's quick and stocks are moving all over the place, that's when we make the most money. Good traders don't have an opinion; we have a feel for the stock and for how it is trading.

By a "feel" for the stock, does that mean you understand where it's come from?

Where it's come from, the price levels. You've been watching it for the past half hour, and hopefully you can make an educated decision on where it's going in the next minute. So then I'll take a big short position in the stock, thinking this is the top. And sometimes I'll be wrong. It happens to everybody. I'll get upset. I'll continue trading but not like I did before. Where before I might short 10,000 or 15,000 shares, I'll sit back on the next trade and maybe do 2000 shares. You can't let one trade change your whole game plan. Stick to your rules, but consider getting smaller when things aren't working the way you planned.

It's possible to make a lot of money quickly in day trading, but it's hard slogging through trade after trade. Thirty highly charged minutes in front of a computer screen can really work up a sweat.

And you can blow it or double it on one trade. You can get ahead of yourself in this game, and it's dangerous to get cocky. But I've had times where for an hour I could do no wrong. I'm trading a stock and 99 percent of the trades are good, they're all for 3000 or 5000 shares, and I'll make 10 grand. Then I'll overextend myself and maybe buy 10,000 or 15,000 shares, fighting the trend just because I know the stock has hit a support level. Then it blows through that support and I can't get out without losing half a point or a buck. That move could undo half of what it took me an hour to make. When that happens, you've just got to sit back, take a deep breath, get a glass of water, and get back in.

It sounds like you've had recurring bouts of overconfidence in your trading career. As you mentioned, it's dangerous to get cocky.

It's not overconfidence. I get stubborn. On my biggest down days, the reason I lost is not because of a bad trade or something stupid; it's because I was stubborn. I refused to cover my position, whether I was long or short, thinking that I'm right and the market is wrong. Once you start thinking like that, it's over. You're done.

You're cooked—at least on that trade.

And probably for the rest of the day. It's hard to fight your way back, especially on a slow day. You start looking for home-run trades. That's when you really put yourself in the hole.

Traders are always warning others not to swing for the fences, but you all do it. That's part of the thrill. On down days, what's wrong with trying to belt out a few home runs and rebound in a big way?

Because instead of making eighths and quarters—what we're trained to do—you're looking to make a half on 8000 shares. On a day when nothing is going on, it's not going to happen. You can make eighths and quarters all over the place, but that big home-run trade just isn't there. Stubbornness is definitely a drawback, and it happens to the best of traders. It's something you have to control.

Have you reached a point now in your trading where you can recognize stubbornness when it happens and shut it down?

I'd like to say I can. The fact that I don't have an opinion of the market is good. I just trade. I'm not here for long-term positions. If six months from now it's doubled in price, that means nothing to me. I'm not here to hold it for six months.

If anything, you hold a stock for six minutes. What's an example of a recent trade where confidence, discipline, and skill came together for a brief, shining moment?

I was on vacation in North Carolina. I took my laptop and modem and traded from there. One day the market opened up huge. Dell, Microsoft, the whole market, was way up. I got in and bought 1000 shares of Dell just to feel it out. Is it strong? Is it weak? You have to be in a stock to really get a feel for it. When you see your profit and loss statement actually up $500 or down $1000, it definitely becomes more real. So I bought 1000 shares and it just didn't feel strong. Dell had opened up about three points, but it didn't feel like it had the oomph to keep going. So I shorted it. Ten minutes later I had made a buck on it. That was a pretty sweet trade.

Dell had opened big; the market was roaring. And you went short?

It didn't feel like Dell was going to keep going through its high. There were so many people long in the stock overnight—institutions, market makers, other traders. Everybody took profits. I got lucky and hit some big bids. I was trying to short as much as I could, but once it turned there weren't many plus ticks.

How could you possibly have known that Dell's stock price would turn in your favor? Do traders just develop a sixth sense after a while?

You can't explain that gut feeling when you know a stock is a short or a long. It's experience, a feel for the stock. I've been trading Dell for two years. I'm not saying I know where it's going to trade today or tomorrow, but I do have a feeling when it opens. I can tell if traders are going to take profits. There's no science to it—if there was, we'd all be millionaires.

What if you had been wrong about the stock and the trade went against you? Wouldn't it have been difficult to get out?

If I was wrong, I wouldn't have a hard time covering because there were lots of guys that I could buy from. I wouldn't lose more than ⅛ or ¼, even ⅜. Although the stock opened up three points and pulled in ¼ and then made a new high by ¼, there were lots of guys selling at the offer. The market makers—Goldman Sachs, Deutsche Morgan Grenfell, First Boston, Merrill Lynch, Morgan Stanley—were offering stock at every level. I just happened to have gotten off my short before they really hit the stock.

I got lucky, and luck is a big factor. If I had missed that one level, that one uptick ⅛ off the top, I wouldn't have been able to do anything because you're not allowed to short on downticks. The stock just dropped from there. There was no shorting it after that. It was all down, down, down. Then it rallied ⅛, rallied ¼, and then down another ½, and I covered. I was short at $120. I covered at $119. The stock actually hit $117½. So I did well, but if I had had more patience, more resilience, I would have made a lot more money. But I was on vacation and the trade was worth nine grand—I'll take that any time.

How many stocks do you follow at once?

I used to follow 120 stocks, and it became very difficult. I cut it down to 40 or 50 stocks. Some traders have 300 stocks they watch; some have 10. I'm finding you have to be a lot more selective and patient. There is more competition now, so I am focusing on fewer stocks.

Has narrowing your watchlist made you a better trader?

I don't know if it's made me a better trader, but it's made me more profitable.

In this game, you need focus. You also need speed, right?

Speed is crucial. You have to be fast. You have to be aggressive; you have to buy stock before other people do. If you don't, you're not going to get any.

Is it a disadvantage if you're not so quick on the keyboard?

If you're not fast on the keyboard on the big days—on the quick-moving stocks—that, I think, is a disadvantage. Still, you have to be a trader before you're a typist.

And focusing on a few stocks might sharpen both your trading edge and your speed.

When we find one stock that's crazy—that is just trading dollars every tick—that's what we'll trade. I won't even look at anything else. Not long ago there was a stock called Entremed, ENMD, that opened up like 70 points one morning, came in 40, ran up another 20. I didn't trade any other stock that day. That stock was a gold mine.

Wasn't it difficult to get shares of such a volatile, high-flying stock?

That's where speed comes into play. I was always able to buy, sell, get in or out, though not at the absolute top or bottom. I don't remember how much I made—I did really well though. You just have to be faster than the next guy.

You have to be quick on the draw. Traders must've been falling over themselves to get into the kind of action that Entremed promised.

A lot of traders actually won't play a stock like that because the stakes are so high. That day, your risk was three or four points. New guys aren't going to risk losing three grand, although your upside was huge—a good 10 points if you caught a big movement. Trading was so fast. And the levels—the stock is offered at $50. The next level, it's offered at $51. So if you missed the $50 stock, right away you're paying $51. If you missed $51, you're paying $52. There is no $50⅛, $50⅜, $50½. Intel is trading eighths and quarters at a time. This was trading dollars. It was crazy. And if you're wrong, it's the same thing to the downside. You try to hit the $49 bid; maybe you sell at $48. If you miss those, you hope to get $47. It's dangerous.

How did you know when trading this stock had become as good as it gets?

You hit a point where you are just trading and paying spreads and not making money either way. It slowed down around noon, picked up again from 2:30 P.M. to 3 P.M., and was dead in the last hour. Although we traded it, we just churned ourselves. The only guys making money then were the market makers.

You once kept a diary. Do you still?

No.

Why not?

The mistakes I make now are pretty much when I get stubborn. It's not like I'm trading badly—my timing is still there. It's just that I get stubborn. I know what I'm doing right when I make money.

One person's stubbornness is another's strong conviction. Either way, traders have to dart in and out of positions,

not get entrenched in them. What happened the last time you took a big bite out of a stock that proved hard to swallow?

I had 4000 shares of a stock—FAMCK is the symbol; I don't even know what it does. No one in my office traded it because it was four points wide with low volume. But the stock looked good on the chart and it seemed there were buyers. So I bought my first thousand at $58, the second thousand at $62, a third thousand at $66, and the fourth at $68. So I already had 10 points of profit by the time I bought my fourth. The stock went to $72, but it was four points wide and I couldn't sell anywhere near the offer. There were just no buyers. When a stock is four points wide, you're going to be very reluctant to hit the bid because that's four points you're giving up. It's a huge spread, because of the lack of liquidity in the stock.

"FAMCK" is the Federal Agricultural Mortgage Corp., also known as "Farmer Mac."

It did very little volume—2000 to 15,000 shares a day, if that. It may have only ticked on my screen three times a day. If you're wrong, you're dying. Mind you that I've got 10 points profit on one of them, but I've got two near the top. The stock is trading $68 bid by $72 offer. All of a sudden one afternoon, they kill it. For no reason. The stock goes from $67 bid, $71 offer to like $54 bid, $58 offer. And I sold 2 points off the bottom. I didn't know what to do. I was a deer in headlights. There was no liquidity and a $2 spread between bids. So there is a market maker bidding $67 for 200 shares and bidding $65 for 500 shares, and another market maker bidding $63 for 500 shares. I couldn't get out even if I wanted to. These market makers are devils. I blew like $30,000 that day. So I got out of the position, and the next day it opened up like 5 points. It was a learning lesson. You win some, you lose some. I didn't lose any sleep over it. You come back and fight the next day. If you're going to cry over money you've lost, this business isn't for you.

You said the charts looked good on that stock.

I was watching it every day for a couple of months. It was up and down, but it felt like there was support at the $55 level. I started buying at $58 and did fine. I tried to sell it at $70 or $71, at or near the offer, but there were no buyers. Nobody wants to pay that kind of spread. I figured the stock might come in 4 or 5 points on me and maybe I would buy another one. But they killed it. I couldn't believe it.

Why not just stick with the tried and true—tick trading— where you're flipping for quarters and halves?

You trade Dell, you're going to make a quarter on 5000. Trade stocks like FAMCK and you're looking at 2, 3, 5, 10 points. But you can't do it in five minutes. It took me two weeks to build that position.

You've had two incarnations in this business. First was from clerk to trader. Then you evolved from a sometimes profitable trader to a consistently winning one. Can you point to one attribute that might explain why you've done so well?

I always limited my downside. I don't wait until I'm really wrong—I try to admit it right away so I don't lose more than a quarter or a half point. It's hard to make money. There is no reason to lose when you could avoid losing. Some guys are reluctant to admit they are wrong until they are really wrong. I never want to be that guy.

Was there a single moment when you knew you'd graduated from being an average trader into the big leagues?

It's so gradual you can't even feel it. Because once you start making money you think, "I'm just getting lucky, let's see if I can keep doing it." You're really not even making money. You're just not losing anymore. You're breaking even. You're not a good trader yet, but you're not a bad trader anymore. From here you just keep on going. I still feel like I'm learning every day.

You have to choose the right moment to jump in and out of a trade. Are these successful plays due more to luck than skill?

It's both. There's no 100 percent guarantee. You take a position. The thing is that when you're wrong, you have to get out right away. If you're wrong, don't be stubborn and say, "How can I be wrong? I'm right." Don't think the stock is wrong, or the market is wrong, or the guys who are buying the stock are wrong. You start that and you're going to get hurt. Although it looks like a big video game, that stuff is cash.

This isn't play money.

I tell that to new guys all the time. When I go over their trades, I ask them, "Did you need to lose $1 in this stock? Could you have gotten out without losing $1?" They always say, "I thought it would rally, and then I sold at the bottom." There's no reason for that. They just don't get it. They don't understand that *it's real money, it's not a game.* They should be cutting their losses. These new guys are making ¼, ⅛, and ⅜ when they're right, but on their downside they are losing dollars. They're killing themselves. I try to explain that to them. I'll say, "When's the last time you made a dollar?" And they say, "We haven't." That's right. Keep doing it this way and you'll keep losing dollars, not making them. Discipline is very big. *The point here is don't lose more on your losers then you make on the winners.*

Day traders love to see high volatility in the market, where shares change hands quickly and stocks bounce in a wide range. That's when you can make the most money. But how do you play days with low volatility?

You sit back and take whatever profit you can. You look for eighths and quarters. And you try not to load up on any one stock, because it's hard to see the trend, if there even is one.

What I like to do on low-volatility days is trade like a market maker, buying on bids on the pullbacks and selling on offers during the rallies. When a stock runs up ½ or ¾, I'll short it on the offer and wait for it to pull in and make ¼ or ⅜ on a couple of thousand shares. What I find works best is to sit back and not force it, to be disciplined, and to look for opportunities. Opportunity is always there. It's a question of waiting and looking for it.

Waiting for opportunity requires patience. Looking for it demands discipline. How are you able to incorporate both qualities into your trading?

Some guys like to start trading at the open. An aggressive market is the right time to do that, but when the market is choppy and not moving well, you should sit back. Do they really sell? Do they really buy? What is the market telling you? And you decide where to go from there. You shouldn't just shoot from the hip and try to move the market yourself—buy a lot of stock hoping it will go up or sell short a lot of stock hoping it will go down. Just wait and see. If the S&P futures are ticking up big and some stocks are only moving up a little, when the futures settle down you might want to short one of those stocks. And if the futures are really selling off, but a stock is hanging in, that's a stock you might want to build a long position in if the futures turn. Because when they turn, this is the first stock that market makers, institutions, and traders will come for.

Other professionals will come for the stock, as you say. but they'll demand the best price. Wall Street is not going to hand over a couple of grand and say, "Here—you deserve this." What tricks have you learned to outfox the pack?

Don't fight the tape; the trend is your friend; limit your losses; let your winners run. It sounds really basic, but it works. New traders should not bottom-fish. I bottom-fish all the time and make a lot of money at it when I'm right. I've lost lots of money at it, too. Bottom-fishing, selling strong stocks, and buying weak stocks is a very dangerous game. It's hard to pick bottoms and to find tops. So buy the strong and sell the weak.

It's when the strong turn weak and the weak turn strong that separates good traders from mediocre traders. That's when you have to figure it out. If you can see that trend before the other guys, and you can pick up a few thousand shares before anyone else, you're going to be selling to everyone else at a half point higher.

Winning—especially a big win—must be a tremendous feeling. There must be a lot of high-fives going around the office.

Not really. I try to keep a straight face whether I'm down $10,000 or up $50,000. You try to control your emotions. If you're up $30,000 and the guy next to you is down $10,000, that's no fun. You don't want to celebrate. You don't want to rub it in. You don't want to gloat. It's business; that's it.

Day trading is a living, to be sure—and an extremely good one for some. But is day trading just a momentary flash, soon to burn out and fade away?

This is a revolution. This is a career of a new generation. Day trading is the wave of the future. It's electronic, it applies to the Internet, everybody's got a PC, and pretty much anybody can do it. You don't need a license. The next step is high-speed connectivity from home. Today you still don't have the speed. We'll see what happens in five years.

Day trading is increasingly popular, but the career of a new generation? In a bear market, many people who depend on Wall Street for a paycheck will be forced to generate a new career.

What's going to happen to guys like me in a bear market? I don't know. But if a stock is down 10 points, that's just as good for me as if it's up 10 points. As long as we have momentum and volatility, we'll make money.

Roy Sidikman
Be Flexible

"There is no bad market, there are only bad price levels."

D ay traders are not investors. They don't concern themselves with cash flow, debt levels, and other traditional
measures of corporate worth. *Day traders care about stock
prices, not valuation.* To a trader, "value" means getting stock
at an eighth or a sixteenth of a point better than someone else.
That price advantage puts an extra few bucks in your pocket
when you sell it a few minutes later. Then it's on to the next
trade.

Many experienced investors think they can shift easily
into day trading because they know about stocks and markets.
But the transition is hardly so effortless. Roy Sidikman is a
sharp, quick-thinking 27-year-old who graduated from college
a year early and soon afterward became a stockbroker. Being
a stockbroker is demanding work. You analyze, agonize, listen, and sell—and that's just with clients. But you do learn
about stocks and markets. Sidikman quickly amassed a great

deal of insight and appreciation for the patterns and behavior that stocks often exhibit.

After two years, Sidikman decided to try another line of work, though he knew it would be stock-related. A friend was doing quite well for himself as an electronic day trader, which in 1995 was still an obscure corner of the market, even among the professional trading crowd. Sidikman had never traded before, but he felt that his strong background in stocks and a good command of industry sectors would be an advantage. So he collected $50,000 between his savings and a loan from his father, and sat down one morning to trade in front of a computer screen at the small firm in New Jersey where his friend worked.

Six weeks later, more than half of his money was gone.

At that point, many newcomers would lick their wounds and sulk away. Not Sidikman. He fought his way back, carefully. In the process he learned to be flexible, no matter the circumstances. And his previous stock market experience and knowledge was valuable, for it gave him the confidence to push ahead. As a result, Sidikman was able to keep his footing on the steep and slippery trail from investor to trader. He's never looked back.

■   ■   ■

Your beginnings as a day trader were just like that of most others—humble. In your case, losing $30,000 in six weeks put this edgy business in perspective. But unlike many new day traders, you had plenty of market experience as a retail stockbroker. What happened?

I know a lot about the market, but in the electronic day-trading world, sometimes you see too much. You get information overload, where you see every single tick, every little move, and you lose the big picture. Day trading is a game, and the top players have a great feel for the market. It cost me money to learn the game. New traders should expect to lose $20,000 to $30,000. In the beginning I was buying stocks at the top and selling them at the bottom, just following the sheep. *But now when everybody is panicking out, I'm looking to buy while it's cheap, or when it's running and everybody is trying to buy, I'm selling when it's expensive.*

Now you're an experienced day trader. That's quite different from being an experienced stock picker; one does not necessarily complement the other. How were you able to stay in the game?

I ended up losing more than half of my equity and had to borrow more money. From there I just started to grind it out. Since then I've only had one losing month in over two years. In the beginning I used to trade a lot of smaller stocks and was happy to make $500 a day. Then I started trying to consistently make $1000 a day. And then slowly my $1000 days became $2000 days, and my good days started becoming $10,000.

How have you been able to progress as a trader? What skills are you implementing better to boost your paycheck?

It was a combination of pressing my winners more and cutting my losers quicker. Now I'm going to buy as much as I can when a stock is cheap. And if I get a good price, I'm going to let that trade ride a bit. An example would be Dell Computer, down $5 a share at one point today. It was cheap, and the market was turning around. In the old days I might buy a thousand or two, wait for it to start working, and then maybe buy another thousand and close it out. Today I was trying to buy as much as I possibly could. I tried to leverage myself. I knew it was cheap and I ended up getting 15,000 shares.

I made about $3—about $45,000—on that one trade. That was pretty much my whole day. In the past I used to be more of a grinder, flipping for sixteenths, eighths, quarters. I do still, that's a very big part of my trading. But when I've got a good feel for a stock, I'm going to try to make $1 or $2 on a trade versus a quarter or an eighth.

And the way that we as day traders can make money is exponential, because if I make $500 today, I have an extra $1000 of buying power tomorrow—there's a two-to-one marginability. So if I make $1000 today, I have $2000 more buying power tomorrow. If at the end of the month I'm up $20,000, I can now buy 1000 shares of a $40 stock. Instead of being able to afford 1000 shares of Dell, I can afford 2000 shares. And as I got better at making money, my buying power got larger, to the point where I can buy 10,000 or 15,000 shares of Dell and really take advantage of a move. That's the main reason why I can make more money now.

How many stocks do you follow at one time?
About 120.

And is that knowledge equally divided among the group, or do you focus on a core?
A core group of 20 to 30 I know like the back of my hand.

Now you might pocket $1000 on a trade, let alone in a day. Was there a specific point in your trading where you cata-

pulted to a higher and more sophisticated level, or has the transformation been more gradual?

One day—October 28, 1997—was the turning point in my career.

That was no ordinary day. The Dow Jones Industrial Average had plummeted about 550 points on October 27. The mood was grim, but stocks finished up sharply the following day.

That was a time when I was still happy to make $500 a day. The market opened down huge. I started buying into some stocks that I never had traded before—crazy highflyers that would move dollars in a second. On that day, just because they were down so much and everybody was buying them, I jumped in. The next thing you know they started running. I ended up making $30,000 that day. It changed my trading forever.

How so? Didn't you just count the day as lucky and go back to your usual ways?

That day stepped me up to the big boys' league. It enabled me to trade larger-capitalization stocks—Intel, Microsoft, Dell, Amazon.com—which have more risk but also greater volatility. And for day traders, the more volatility, the more money you can make. And not only did I now have confidence in trading these high-flying stocks, but I made $30,000, so I was willing to risk a few thousand dollars the next day. It got me over the hump. What hurts a lot of newer traders is they just can't get over the hump. That big day changed my life. It changed me from trading scared to being aggressive.

How would you describe the difference between fearful and aggressive trading?

In the beginning, I would see a stock like Intel running up and I would hesitate, thinking that I'm chasing it. I'm already up $500, and I don't want to lose a quarter of a point. That was trading scared—when you hesitate buying because you don't want to lose. Now if I think Intel is going to go, I'm going to be aggressive. If it goes against me a bit, big deal. Maybe I'll flip the other way and go short. In fact, now I'm afraid not to enter the trade because maybe I'm going to miss a run in the stock.

Being aggressive has been rewarding for you, both financially and professionally?

Absolutely. You can never have too much of a stock that is going in your direction, knowing that as soon as the stock bases out and starts turning up, there is going to be a lot of interest. If I can find the point where it has bottomed out, where it becomes oversold, I've got an advantage.

But where is the advantage when other traders are seeing the same price movement and share volume that you are?

Sometimes you don't even think; you just know. It's a gut feeling. I'm not smarter than the analysts. I'm just looking for the sellers to dry up and more people to bid for the stock. Then the trade is not as risky as it was, since you're no longer trying to catch a falling knife.

What are some major clues to finding strong stocks? Maybe the stock doesn't break through a downside resistance level, or a couple of market makers flip to the bid side.

Exactly. You start seeing market makers step in and you can almost feel them saying this is getting too cheap. And you also see bids building on the ECN—electronic communications networks—as others look to buy into the dip. That's what I'm looking for.

Are you able, through your positions, to directly impact the price of a stock?

There are times when a stock is pulling back and I will personally try to hold it—buying 20,000 or 25,000 shares. I'll put a bid in, knowing that I have support a few levels beneath. I become more of a market maker, because I buy strong stocks on pullbacks and fade out of them on rallies. Like today, I bought the 15,000 Dell, and when it was running up I slowly offered. I'd go maybe a sixteenth below the offer the whole way up, and fade out of it just like a market maker would.

I'll dollar-cost average into a good position, too. If, for instance, Dell is pulling in, I'll bid a thousand at one level, and another thousand at another level. Then it stops. It looks like it's bottomed out and started to turn up. Then I try to buy 2000 or 3000 more. The stock runs up, and I fade out of half my position right away and make all the money back. If it's still a strong position, I'm going to capitalize on it with that other half. I'll ride it a little further. I bought three at the bottom and just made a half. Now I have a little cushion in the trade, and maybe this is going a lot higher.

So a day trader actually doesn't need wide spreads to make money?

No. It doesn't make any difference. The whole NASDAQ market itself has been evolving toward tighter spreads and more liquidity. You've just got to buy stocks at good levels. Levels and prices are very important. *There is no bad market, there are only bad price levels.*

What do you mean by a "bad" level?

The hardest part for new people is everybody says, "The market is bad. Nothing is happening. Stocks are just in a range." But I can still make money in a bad market if I know my levels well. If I'm buying at the high, I'm in a lot of trouble. That's how new people get hurt. As long as I'm buying stocks near the bottom and selling them near the top, I'm still going to make money no matter what the market is doing. Some people call this the market-maker game; it works for me.

As you watch a stock move up and down through its levels, what are you looking for? You want to enter the trade at the right point, but how do you know when a stock is meeting overhead resistance—it can't get through a level—and when it's poised to break out?

I look at the momentum of the stock. If a stock is falling down hard and it approaches a support level, I might wait and not be the first bidder. If it looks like it can fall further, I might get short. It all depends on how quickly I see buyers and sellers come into the market. If there's support at $105, for example, I'm going to bid it an eighth or a sixteenth higher because maybe the whole world is bidding $105 and I'm never going to get any stock. I'll cut off the pack, taking an eighth of a point pain just to get into my trade. If I can hold the position and the S&P futures start turning my direction, my bid becomes the support level and the price never even goes lower.

So thanks in part to you, all those $105 orders don't get executed.

Well, that may be true, but that's what makes a market. I was willing to pay the best price. The next thing you know, the $105 bids are paying ⅜ and I'm making seven teenies and half sales to others.

Trading larger, "market" stocks like Dell and Intel involves a certain set of rules and strategies. How about small stocks? What are some ways you've discovered to play those?

In smaller stocks, I look for a lot of volume. I have about 50 smaller stocks on my ticker, and what I'm looking for is movement that I normally don't see. These little stocks don't trade much. But when one breaks a high on the day, I want to be involved. Usually there is a news story or something going on in the sector.

With small stocks, I've noticed, the market makers have a lot more say in what's going to happen. With a stock like Dell, Intel, Microsoft—I don't care if Bear Stearns has a million-share sell order, if the market is rallying back, the stock is going higher. In a small stock, one firm could stay there with a large order and the stock will not move no matter what. There just isn't enough interest. A lot of games go on. There also are games in the bigger stocks, of course, but Goldman Sachs is not going to stop a freight train. If Dell is screaming up and announces a two-for-one split, I don't care how many shares he has to sell, eventually he's going to dry up and the stock is going higher. In smaller stocks that's not always true.

What's nice about smaller stocks is that new traders can leverage them. They can afford to buy 5000 shares of a $6 stock because you're only tying up $30,000 of buying power. In a stock like Intel, they can only afford 1000 shares, if that.

Aren't small stocks riskier to trade?

No. A quarter-point move in a $5 stock is the same as a quarter-point move in $100 stock. It doesn't make that big a difference. And usually they are easier to trade because Goldman Sachs and Merrill Lynch have their best traders on Microsoft, Intel, Dell, and the like. Their newer guys are trading these little companies. They have tricks, too, but they're easier to play against.

You mentioned that market makers play games with traders. What are some of their best tricks?

Suppose you see Goldman Sachs go high bid for Intel. But you know what? By him going high bid, that might mean the stock is going lower. He's buying it, trying to hold it up, but he might be selling more shares through other firms or through ECNs.

And what market makers are very good at, the biggest trick of them all, is making stocks look their best before they make them move in the other direction. If Dell is running, they are going to push Dell up until it looks like that stock is going to $150 a share and every last short covers. As soon as everyone gets long, that's when the market makers flip and the stock drops $2. It's amazing how they know the tolerance of pain for people and how they make things look that much better at the top. As soon as it looks too good, it usually is.

That's why I short a strong rally at the top, because odds are that a lot of people are getting long, a lot of the shorts are covering, and you know the market makers are going to sell more and bring it down and buy their stock back. These market makers are shorting into these rallies also. They have to fill their clients. If the stocks run too far, they are not going to go out and buy the stock. They're going to sell it short in their own account, knowing they can buy it on a pullback from all the rookies who bought at the high. It's just games they play—games they are good at.

What tactics can a trader use to beat the market makers at their own game?

To beat them, you have to follow them. When I fade in and out of positions, I'm following their game, shadowing them, but my advantage is that I don't have to do the size they do. I can be a lot more agile.

But sometimes the market makers sting you.

Sure. I remember buying Dell around $100 a share and getting jiggled out at around $99¼. The stock hit 98¾, and I blinked. But I couldn't buy my shares back because the stock was moving so fast. The next thing you know it's trading $105.

You got shaken out of the position and then lost the chance to get back in before it rebounded.

It broke a support level and I just couldn't take the pain.

How do you react to losing trades like that? Do you rant and rave, or just dust yourself off and move on?

You took a shot. If you're a good trader and you get jiggled out, you might buy back the stock higher—but you're going to buy it back.

What do the market makers hope to gain from your pain?
They just want to fill their orders at the best available price for their clients. If they're sellers, they want to sell that stock as high as they can. If they're buyers, they want to buy as cheaply as they can. They are going to move out of the way and even sell a little bit trying to buy it cheaper.

With buy orders in hand, the market makers try to build selling pressure, hoping to drive the stock price down and then fill their long positions. They'll do just the opposite on the other side of a trade.
Exactly. It's a game where you have to put the pieces together, use all the clues, and make your best bet. You've got to be smart and quick. Then you have to admit when you're wrong.

Admitting a mistake is difficult for many people, and day traders are no exception. What's your excuse?
Because even when you're wrong, you're thinking, I've held this $1 against me—it's got to go up. Then you start looking at the fundamentals of a company, hoping to justify your position. That's wrong. Valuation should mean nothing. When I start worrying about valuation and start looking too deeply into a company, I'm not doing what I'm here to do. I'm here to trade.

Is it a natural inclination of people to analyze?
I do it all the time.

So part of being a good trader is avoiding what's often called the "paralysis of analysis." But people always like to examine the merchandise before they buy. What key lesson have you learned that allows you to be more of an impulse buyer?

Be flexible. *Every day I adapt to the market.* What kind of style is going to make me the most money today? Is it just flipping in and out? Is it bidding in heavy at a certain level and then trying to go for the big move? Each day is different.

Some days you hit singles and doubles; others bring the home runs.

There are days when losing $1000 is a good day. The best traders can recognize if it's a good day or a bad one. Is the risk/reward there? A big problem with newer traders is they make $2000 on a better day, then lose $4000 with commissions on a bad day. The better traders recognize this is a crummy day and there's no reason to take big shots. And many newer traders can't take advantage of days when there's a lot of money to be made. They're happy being up $2000 or $3000, and they're not aggressive enough. Look at it this way: there are going to be days when you lose. So when there's money to be made and the market is meant for traders, you've got to be aggressive, because we might not see another day like that for six months.

What kind of day offers a market made for traders?

A market of big intraday reversals and big moves across large ranges. When there's a small range on the stock and low volume, you don't have an edge. Then you're trading as little as possible, waiting for that big move. If it doesn't happen, don't get involved. *You've got to press on the days when the money is there.* Because making $5000 in a day is still a losing day if there was $10,000 to be made. I want to make as much money as possible that day. *And when there is no money to be made, I'm not going to force myself to make it.*

How do you quantify the risk and reward of a particular day? What scale helps you weigh the odds and decide what kind of day it is?

I ask myself, is there money to be made trading right now? If I don't see stocks ripping one way or another—when things are stuck in their range—there is not a lot of reward there because I'm paying the spread; I'm paying the big commission. But when you see something that's either cheap to buy or so overpriced that you want to short, you've got to jump all over it. The key here is to be disciplined enough to get out if the trade goes against you.

In time, it seems a trader gets to know the personalities of these stocks. You study them. They take on a life of their own. You know how much they typically run in a day, and act accordingly if prices move too far in one direction.

That's exactly the way it is. Every stock is different, and every stock has its day. Some stocks are in play every day, and some only once a month. Maybe it's a cyclical stock. I used to make a lot of money trading oil driller stocks. They used to be on fire. Then they became stuck in a range—they wouldn't move more than a half point a day, so I didn't even waste my time with them. But when they were in play, I was in them.

Much has been made—both praise and criticism—of the influence that day traders exert on share volume and

prices. How do you assess your role and the power of day trading to move markets?

Day trading causes more volatility. Say Merrill Lynch has an order to buy one million shares of Intel, and both Intel and the market are strong. You know what? I'm buying Intel. I see it's strong, it's not pulling back, and my buying it forces them to move to a higher bid until they eventually can find sellers. So we're moving stocks until there are natural sellers. In essence, we are costing these mutual funds money, because they might be paying a little higher for a stock position than they normally would have. On the other hand, we save the small investor money by narrowing spreads.

Yet day traders thrive on market volatility, and the sheer volume of day-trading activity serves to heighten the big price swings. Let's talk about ways to use volatility to your advantage. How, for instance, do you navigate a swift current where the market is moving quickly to the upside or the downside?

The number one rule in day trading is short a gap up opening and buy a gap down opening. Today, stocks gapped up, then sure enough, the market screamed down negative. I didn't short because I thought we were going to bounce back. Then stocks found support and started turning higher. That's when I started loading up.

I could have made a lot of money going short, but I was more concerned about getting long at the bottom. My gut feeling was the market was going to rally. So instead of getting short, I was waiting for the momentum on the downside to slow, and then to start bidding when the market firmed up. The market was still going down as I was buying, but I knew that the only way to get into these stocks was to take a little pain. You've got to get stock when you can, at the levels you can, because once they start turning, there is no buying them. Everybody in the world wants them. Sellers move out of the way and the stocks just move dollars.

What strategy works for you on days when the market is giving traders a roller-coaster ride, whipping them up, down, and around?

I lock in profits. As soon as I see the momentum slowing down, as soon as I see offers coming in, I'll go a sixteenth or an eighth lower than everybody else, even if the stock is still going up. As it slows down, I'm offering into the rally. And when a strong stock pulls in, I'm bidding into the pullback. I fade in and out of positions. I'll get short, the stock pulls in. I'll bid them all back and ride the rally.

So in a hairpin market, you cut corners early. Let the other guy hit the wall. If volatility is a trader's best friend, then those calm, sideways markets must be extremely frustrating.

Those are my worst days. Slow-bleed days are the hardest. You end up paying the spreads because there is not a large enough range on the stocks. So what happens is a stock might run ⅜ of a point, pull in ⅛ or ¼, run ⅜, pull in ¼, and every time it runs you think it's going to explode, so you buy a lot. Then it starts ticking down—you've bought the high. Then you sell it out, it starts going back up, and you're thinking, "I gave it away." It gets very choppy on the slow-bleed days; they are difficult to trade. They're great days for playing market maker, buying the pullbacks, and selling the rallies.

Do you do trade on news?

Yes. Anywhere I think I have an edge over anybody else in trading is where I want to be. Sometimes on a good news story, you have an edge. Trading news is an art in itself. A lot of new traders get beat up real bad on news because a stock runs up and they buy the top. Then it starts pulling in and they sell the bottom. If a great news story comes out, I try to buy it right away. But if I don't get it, I let it run. As soon as I see it getting heavy on the offer side, I hit every plus tick there is and get short. A lot of times stocks end up going lower on good news because people sell into it. But new traders ought to keep away from news stories and tips. Those are the two biggest killers in the beginning.

How do you gain an edge on a news story? You're hearing information at the same time as everyone else.

Our true edge is that we're faster. By the time the average retail client wants to buy that stock, I could have already bought and sold it five times. First you've got to dial the phone, call your broker, he writes down the trade, he looks in your account and makes sure there is enough equity, and then the trade is put in. We are buying the stocks sometimes quicker than the market makers themselves.

And speed, after all, is basically the ball game.

It's all a game. It's a bunch of pretty colors on a screen. I don't even know what I do anymore. I just hit buttons and make money. It's amazing what we do. I never thought that I could possibly make what I do today. And there is nothing I would rather do than day trade.

Marc Sperling
Book Profits

"You've got to think about it as a business."

With its minute-by-minute focus, a day trader's world is intensified in ways that a buy-and-hold investor would find difficult to comprehend. Most investors over time enjoy long, profitable bull markets and endure periodic, painful bear markets. Not day traders. They see market movement in real time. In day trading, a bull market is when a stock runs three points in 30 minutes. If it's down three, that's a bear market. Traders traverse these bullish and bearish sands several times in a day.

Before Marc Sperling started day trading, he was a stockbroker, seeing the market with the same long-term perspective that he tried to instill in his clients. He learned through trial and error that to a day trader, "long term" is holding a position through lunch; traditional, methodical views of stock selection simply don't work in an electronic game where reflexes often count for more than research.

Sperling has developed a personal trading edge that is full circle from the button-down brokerage business he left behind. The 27-year-old plays a momentum game, climbing onto volatile, fast-moving stocks and jumping off quickly either to book a fast profit or keep a loss small. He plugs away, fingers flying on the computer keyboard, doggedly making fractional gains that soon can add up to real money. His computer screen displays his profit and loss for the day, and Sperling watches that figure intently. He has a monetary goal he wants to reach, a minimum to make for the day. If he soars above that, terrific. But he fights hard not to drop below his bottom line.

Here's a tip from Sperling on how to be a successful day trader. *Book your profits. Don't give back your gains,* he warns.

Give back profits? Sounds ridiculous, doesn't it? If someone does a few hours' work and makes $100, would he hand the cash back to his employer? Of course not. But day trading isn't all in a day's work. This is not an hourly job; there's no guaranteed salary and performance bonus. You're on your own, and though day traders wouldn't have it any other way, this independence can also breed overconfidence. Your goal is to make $1000 a day, but it's late morning and already you're up $3000. Today's your lucky day; obviously, you have the golden touch. It might not be there tomorrow, so why not go for that extra grand? You're playing with the house's money, so bet the ranch.

As Sperling discovered the hard way, he wasn't playing with "house" money—it was his money. He didn't know his limitations, so he pushed his limit. Many days he'd have a big open, and then, looking for an even bigger score, would give back his gains before lunchtime. Naturally, he'd want to push even harder to make up lost ground. The frustration from this vicious circle grew until Sperling just couldn't take it anymore.

Once he made a conscious effort to understand his mistakes, the answer became clear: *book profits before the market takes them away.*

■   ■   ■

How did you get involved with day trading?

I was a stockbroker for three years—the first two of which I enjoyed. The growth was good and I was learning about the market. But I got tired of dealing with clients and with the hassle of what brokers have to put up with. One of my friends was day trading. It was a bit risky, but at the time—this was September 1996—I was 24 years old. I had made decent money in the market and wanted to take a shot at doing something I actually enjoyed.

Was day trading really so enjoyable at first? From what I understand, learning even the basic skills requires considerable time and frustration—and then it still might not pay off.

I put about $100,000 into the account. But I had a lot of computer mistakes, and I lost $25,000 the first seven weeks. The next six weeks I made all of it back.

That must be some sort of speed record. How were you able to reclaim your fortune after just a few weeks?

By focusing on fewer stocks, taking profits when I had them, and not letting losses go against me.

Most traders log months of tough work and even tougher losses before they gain a foothold.

I caught on quickly compared to the learning curve I see for other people. I had experience trading stocks for my own account. Maybe that sped the process. But day trading has become a lot harder. The learning curve is longer—minimum six months.

Why has day trading become harder?

The market makers have gotten smarter. They know how to deal with us. I've heard that when electronic trading first started in the late 1980s, you would push a SOES button and the market makers would fill you and then lift. You'd make three points in the stock without any stress. Now these market makers know what they are doing. They know how to play the game with you.

What are some tricks that market makers will use to out- fox day traders?

They fake bids. They take stock on the offer—just enough to get orders from people trying to buy—and at the next level they stop it cold on the sell side. They act like they're buyers when they're really sellers. It took them a while to learn how to fool us; now we've got to learn what they're doing. You've just got to learn how to play that game. That takes looking at the stocks. You see a market maker taking stock on the bid. People are hitting him, and he keeps buying as the stock moves up. All of a sudden he flips over—you see him at the offer. Maybe it's only for a second. We know he's just playing around. He's not really a seller. He's still a buyer. He just wants to bring down the price a bit so he can buy more of the stock cheaper.

You're looking at stock prices on a screen, and the move- ment and direction are clues to a bigger picture. It's infor-

mation that helps your decision to buy or sell. But most people would just see bright colors and flashing numbers.

It's just learned as you go. You'll get tricked before you're successful. The market makers have gotten smarter, and the market itself has changed. You used to be able to go long seven or eight different stocks and manage them with no problem. Stocks in the same industry used to move in basically the same direction. Not anymore. Some might lag, some might be weak for the day. You never know. So you've got to manage your positions, and I try not to have too many at the same time.

Managing account positions seems an important responsibility. So does managing emotions. How do you handle that?

Not very well. It's hard. I'm hoping it gets better. *If you can take the emotion out of trading, you'll be a much better trader.* Right now, I'm still trading a lot with emotion.

Does everybody around you know when you're having a bad day?

Per trade, I don't really complain about losing ⅛ or ¼ or ½. At the same time, if I'm in a trade and I know it's going up, and I bang it out before I really want to or I didn't make what I thought I should have, I'm frustrated—why didn't I hold it? That's emotion. And when you have emotion, you get angry and bad things happen.

Emotions have a sinister way of slowly erasing a carefully developed game plan. You lose focus.

You lose complete focus. *You revenge trade, where if you lost money in a stock, you'll try to make it back by doubling the amount of shares you normally would buy. That never works.*

The other day I was long five Internet stocks and the market was down 19 or 20 handles (points) right in the morning. I was down $25,000—the biggest down day I have ever had. I can count on two hands the times I've lost more than $10,000 in a day. Down $25,000. At first I started to take a few shots that I wouldn't normally if I was even. Then I realized I was just being stupid. I started just trying to make a little back one trade at a time, and by the end of the day I was only down $1700.

You encourage people to book profits, and that seems wise. But traders also watch people like you win and lose a few thousand bucks in a morning and wonder how they're ever going to play in that league.

Don't look at everybody else. *Think independently. It is your money that you will make or lose.* It's hard to judge when you see people making thousands of dollars a day and you're like, oh, I made $100. But you've got to be realistic. You've got to have your goals. If you have a goal, say you want to make $10,000 a month, or $500 a day, since there are about 20 trading days in the month. Say you make $1000 and you start giving back, you'd better make sure you stay above $500. You should only give back 20 percent of your daily high. That's hard because you see everybody else trading around you. But that's where discipline comes in. You become a lot more successful at this if you start booking profits early. It's easy to keep trading and churning yourself. It's like playing a video game all day long. Who wants to stop that? But instead of points, it's real money.

I used to make money in the morning and keep churning. I would be up $4000 by 10:15 A.M. and by 11:30 A.M. I would give it all back. I wasn't disciplined and I couldn't even realize what was going on. I just kept trying to push and would never be satisfied. I should have been more in tune with the big picture; $4000 was a pretty good day. Once I recognized that, I was able to take my game to the next level. It was just a matter of trading with a little discipline and recognizing what I was here to accomplish.

It sounds like you were never staying in one place long enough to be satisfied.

When you're not doing well, you're trying to focus on everything. That's impossible. If you follow a few different stocks closely, you know exactly what they're doing. You know your ability, you know you can do the job because you've made money before. It's a matter of fine-tuning and paying attention to detail. In the beginning its best not to shoot too high, limit the number of stocks you follow, and don't get greedy.

Day traders talk about trading with less money and fewer shares to climb out of a slump. Why should you also trim the number of stocks you trade?

I've found that when you take on less, you do better. That's hard, because you're looking at everyone around you. It's a great market, but here you are struggling; you can't really get your groove going. You've got to find what works for you, and do it every time. Don't worry about home runs; just hit the ball. Make singles, and eventually your singles become doubles, those doubles become triples, and the triples become home runs. Consistency is the key.

Apparently it's possible for a day trader to make quite a comfortable living just hitting singles and doubles; you don't ever have to hit a home run.

You should just be a consistent singles and doubles hitter. You'll make more money over the long term, versus somebody who tries to swing for a home run every time. Sure, they'll have their big up days, but they'll have their big down days, too.

Was there a point in your trading where you went from swinging for the fences to appreciating the value of singles and doubles?

When I was getting fed up with making $4000 and then giving it all back. After a while you kick yourself and ask, "What am I doing?" But I'd push it, trying to make that five grand—then end up with $1000 for the day. I got sick of it and started trading smaller. I would book $1000 or $1200 and when I would give back 20 percent, I would stop. I had to get disciplined. And it's hard.

How long did you force yourself to trade in such a strict manner?

At least two or three months. Then you get your confidence back. Once you regain your confidence, it's amazing what you can do. Then you don't even hit the home runs. You realize that singles every day add up to a lot of money at the end of the month and a very good living at the end of the year.

Speaking of making real money, what catalyst do you want to see before initiating a trade?

At the open I look to do the opposite of what the market is doing. Say the market opens higher. I have a list of stocks I look at first, and I go down the order. If the stocks I'm following are coming in, meaning their price is falling, I might try to short them right off the bat to see if I can make a quick ¼ or ⅜. If they don't come in—they hold up—then when the market starts to rise they're the first stocks I buy. Stocks that don't come in when the market is going down are the strong stocks. They'll be the first to rally.

Are there any particular types of stocks or industry sectors that you're more likely to trade?

I always look for the most active stocks. I don't have to know anything about the company; it doesn't matter. Bottom line: You make money as a day trader in the volatile stocks. When they slow down, look elsewhere.

If Internet stocks are active, that is all I look at. You'll also trade what are called the (NASDAQ) "market" stocks: Dell Computer, Intel, Microsoft, Cisco Systems. Another area includes the stocks in the Philadelphia Semiconductor Sector index—the SOX. You trade whatever has been active, but you trade them all differently.

What different strategies do you use to trade Internet stocks, for instance, versus the big NASDAQ market stocks?

The Internet stocks have wider spreads. They can be ½ or ¾ wide. If you are paying the offer on the stock and the stock drops bid, you're down ½ or ¾ before you know it. So you can't take huge positions in them—perhaps a few thousand shares. If the momentum is right, I get rid of one immediately up ⅛ or ¼ higher than my last buy, and by the time the stock runs a half I'm out of another one. I usually hold one to see if it's going to do anything more than run the half. The market stocks you can position-trade—hold them for a few hours.

What's your first move when the opening bell rings?

I've put five to seven stocks on the ticker in the middle of my screen, and it shows me every tick consistently. Everything I need to know is on my screen. The first stocks I look at have been Amazon.com and Yahoo!—two of the wildest Internets. I look at them first because they lead the other Internets.

If I see no one hitting the bid on Amazon and Yahoo!, I'm going to go long as they come in. I make most of my money going long. I buy the bounces rather than short the rallies in most cases. So when these stocks are not going down anymore and the market starts to rally, I will high-bid somebody to see if they'll hit me. If no one hits me, I'll take the offer.

Why are you paying the offer instead of buying on the bid and capturing the spread?

Because the market is starting to rally and these stocks are not pulling in. I want to be the first one in. Then I know I'm making ½ on the stock. Sometimes I'll take as much on the offer as I can. I just want the stock—4000, 5000, 6000 shares. Then you just offer them out sporadically as they're going up. If it runs ¼ you offer one. The stock moves another ⅛, you offer one more. It goes another ⅛, offer another. So within 30 seconds I can make $1000 easily. If I sell them all out and realize the stocks are coming in, I'll go long again. And once the trend is up and the market makers can't really bring the stocks in, I'll hold some of these stocks for points.

What evidence do you have—the proof is all electronic— that a stock isn't going down?

I try to see who has a buy order, who goes high bid, and who's sitting on the bid. If there are a lot of people on the offer and one guy on the bid, I try to see if that guy is a real buyer. There is a lot of scared money playing these stocks—a lot of new people who get jiggled out with the price movements. And don't get me wrong, I do too once in a while. But I feel I've learned how to play those jiggles. It can be 10 seconds for me to switch. I am probably one of quickest people on the keyboard. I have quick fingers. It's an advantage to me because I can type up a stock symbol and can get involved in two different stocks in a few seconds.

It takes you a few seconds to execute a trade for two different stocks?

I can buy two stocks pretty quick, a few seconds at most. Definitely.

That's not much time to form an opinion.

I try not to form a hard-nosed opinion; I'm more reacting to what a stock or the market is telling me. Suppose a newspaper story says that Intel is buying back two million shares. You might think the stock is going to be up five points. If it's already up $2 at the open, I'm not going to believe that the stock will keep going up just because they are buying back shares; then again, maybe it will. It depends on how the stock is acting. When I was a broker I used to just form an opinion: Intel is buying back stock—it must be going higher. That was the hardest thing to learn from when I started as a broker to when I became a trader. As a broker you buy for the long term. It doesn't matter what the little jiggles do. But here it's what these stocks are doing for the next minute or even the next 20 seconds. A strong opinion can really hurt you if you are a trader.

Are there clues about a stock that appear on your computer screen to help you trade faster and not get shaken out of a winning position?

It's just experience. I don't think there is an exact science to trading. One day a stock can be strong, the next day it will be weak. You have to figure out the patterns that go on within the stock. That takes looking at the stock all day long and trying to get in its head. You have to identify a few different factors of what makes the stock.

What is the most important factor, the key ingredient, that helps you assess trading risk?

I look at the spread. How many people are sitting on the bid? Say a stock is $38 by $38½. There are five guys on the bid and two guys at the $38½ offer. The stock looks like it's coming down. I'm willing to risk bidding ⅛ or a teenie because there are five guys I know I can get out with at $38 if I'm wrong. If somebody panics and does hit me at ⅛, and then a bunch of buyers come up ⅛ and the stock starts to rally again, I offer at ⅝ and make ½ just like that—two seconds. That's the advantage of playing market maker. What did I risk? I risked ⅛. What did I make? I made ½.

It sounds simple, but it's hard to grasp. But when you're doing it for a little while, it becomes natural. I didn't learn how to play market maker until probably a year into trading. It was a different market before. You could just take the offer and the stock would go up. Day traders and market makers now are a lot better than they were before. It's survival of the fittest.

So you've put on a good trade, maybe even captured the full spread. What about the times when you miss the tar-

get and buy at a less attractive price? Does both your per-spective and management of a trade change depending on your entry point?

If I have a good entry point—I'm going to hold it longer. If the stock already ran ¼ and I'm paying up ⅜, I might sell out because I don't really know where it came from. I know I paid up a little so if I can make a little, it was a gift for me. Whereas if I had already bought it at $65 and I knew I couldn't get it below $65, I might hold it all day for 1½, 2 points. I've held stocks 8 or 9 points before. But if I didn't have them at a good price, I would never have been able to hold.

And what if the stock just sits there for what seems like an eternity, trapped in a narrow band?

When I first started trading I would have sold the stock. I'd just get frustrated with it. Now I hold it until it moves. But it took me almost two years to reach that point.

During the trading day, you'll take positions of all sizes. When do you know to step on the gas and shoulder more risk?

When you're making money. *When you see your profit and loss statement going up and everything you're doing is right, that's when you press it. When everything is wrong, you don't want to start doubling up.* That's stupid.

Day traders all seem to have a story about the times that everything went wrong—not just in a single trade, but day after day, sometimes for months. It's the nature of the game. But intellectually knowing that you're likely to lose money at first is vastly different from actually feeling that

loss in your gut. How do you know when not to throw in the towel?

When you feel the most pain is when most traders start to turn it around.

It's often said that the point of maximum pessimism, when nobody else believes, is the best time to invest. For a day trader who has been thoroughly beaten, you're investing in yourself just when it seems smart to get an office job.

When you feel like you're at the absolute bottom, where you can't do this any more, where nothing is working, that is when you are going to start to turn around. Everybody who does this is relatively aggressive by nature. When they've lost a substantial amount of money and are at the point of no return, they start to realize, okay, I have to slow down. I have to be patient. I have to look at fewer stocks. That's when they really start to follow the rules. Everybody says they're humble when they first begin, but no one really is. It's just human nature. We're all the same, deep down, in that way. When you're feeling the worst, it usually can only get better, and that's how it is with trading.

But before you make the grade, you get tested.

I was hurting. I could feel the pain. I lost all that money in seven weeks. Damn! How am I going to make a living at this? And the next six weeks I made it all back.

Experience and learning have helped many day traders to develop a personalized, unique style. But a common quality among day traders—and it's striking, really—is a high level of self-awareness and introspection.

Trading is all mental. If you have a positive attitude, it's going to help a lot in trading. It's not going to make you money, but it's going to enable you to at least think clearly. You'll have bumps and bruises along the way. I know I'm going to get another. That's just how it works. But now I'm at a point where if I get a little bump, that's fine. You just have to fight your way through. The hardest thing is thinking of it as trading. *You've got to think about it as a business.* How many businesses become profitable after six months? Very few. In this business you have a chance to become profitable after six months. Some of the better guys have even made six figures the first year, but this is not the norm. Think of it as a regimen you have to stick to. It will make you a better trader.

Eric Fromen
Know Your Levels

"I realized I should not trade a stock unless I know where the stock is coming from."

He's called "Heshy," though Eric Fromen insists it has no special meaning. It's just a nickname that stuck, he says. Fromen is also known as a momentum trader, a quick-on-the-keystroke player who surfs high-flying NASDAQ stocks as they crest and crash throughout a trading day. The raw trading style has stuck to him as well, only this time it means everything.

Fromen paddles out and catches a wave that's building in one of his favorite trading stocks. The surf has been up on Wall Street since he began day trading in 1996. Market volatility—the engine that drives momentum traders—has resurged with a vengeance after being abnormally calm for much of the 1990s. Once he puts on a trade, Fromen hangs tight.

No matter where in the trade he is, Fromen is heavily in risk-control mode, aware of his stock's most recent bid and ask spread and the price support below him if he needs to bail out. This staircase of bid and ask prices is what traders call *levels*.

Nothing is more important to successful day trading than knowing your levels, Fromen contends. When you understand where a stock has been trading, it's an important clue to where it might be going. At what price is a stock meeting overhead resistance? Where is the downside? Which direction is it likely to move when it makes higher highs and higher lows? Knowing a stock's price levels gives a trader a much-welcome comfort level. And in this job, you take whatever you can hold onto.

You might expect a momentum player to radiate kinetic energy, but Fromen, 28, exudes an aloof coolness that passes for attitude among many day traders. Did Fromen make or lose $10,000 today? Talking with him, you'd never know. He's got a look that says, "Trading is my living, not my life. I win big; I lose big. Boom. That's the game."

Is this posture for real? Probably. Day traders guard their anonymity—both during market hours and after the close. No $1000 suits for these folks—too conspicuous and corporate. Let the drones don the Wall Street uniform and toe the company line; day traders cherish their independence. And what better way to declare it than to come to work on sweltering summer days in shorts, tennis shoes, and a T-shirt with a sleeveless sweater pulled over? So you don't look like a million bucks. At least you could be worth it.

■　　■　　■

Day trading has many rules—when to buy, when to sell, how to gain the maximum profit from a position. Anyone can absorb specific information, but each person tailors the rules to his or her own satisfaction. In this way, a

trader develops a personal style, or edge, in approaching the market. How important is a personal edge to trading successfully?

It's absolutely important. Thousands of traders are out there trying to make a living. Probably more of them don't make money than do. If you don't differentiate yourself, you don't get anywhere. You must have an edge or you're not going to make money at this.

Creating that edge is challenging, to be sure. It happens over time—if it comes at all. You try on a few hats before you find one that's comfortable. Perhaps a way to develop a personal style is for a trader to take the lessons learned and prioritize them. That unbreakable rule at the top could shape a cutting edge.

The most important rule of trading is to know your levels on the stocks. When I first started, I would see a stock going up and I would jump on board. I didn't realize what it was doing beforehand. For example, if a stock is trading at $100½ and I see it going up, I might buy it at $100½. But if I wasn't watching its levels, I have no right to buy the stock. How do I know the stock didn't just come from $100 and go to $100½? So all of a sudden, I'm paying up a half point. I'm buying the stock where a lot of people may be selling it already because it already moved.

I remember a more experienced trader walking by me and asking, "What's Intel trading at?" I didn't know. I had to call it up to see. He said that if you're trading Intel or any stock, you should know at all times where it's trading. *That was the key point where I realized I should not trade a stock unless I know where the stock is coming from.*

Traders speak with reverence about knowing a stock's levels. They mean having a crucial and constant awareness of the bid and ask levels at which a stock is hovering. Knowing levels doesn't mean getting a quick quote of where it closed yesterday and opened today. It's watching every tick and seeing the formation as a short-term trading pattern. Can you describe what that looks like from your side of the computer screen?

A trader will watch a stock to see how it acts—it might be only for a few minutes—and he'll realize that here is a stock that has gone from $100 to $100½ and then pulled in. Remember, stocks don't move in straight lines. Stocks go up and pull in, go up and pull in, over and over. Here, you're looking at a stock go from $100 to $100½. It pulls back to $100⅛, then goes up to $100¾.

When a stock is making higher highs and higher lows, you want to wait for it to pull in and try to buy it, then as it goes up try to sell it. What I was doing as a beginner was to watch a stock go up and then buy. It would come in and I would sell. Obviously, that was the wrong way to do it. I was always paying up for stocks, and in my first six months of trading I lost $53,000.

That's painful—$53,000 in capital gone up in electronic smoke. A blow like that doesn't leave you much breathing room.

It hurt a lot. Once I was down $30,000 it hit me that I had to make some money back. That attitude just dug me more into a hole. If you say, "I have to make a certain amount of dollars today" or you say, "Oh my God, how am I going to feed my family? I have to make money," you'll drive yourself crazy. You'll look for home runs all the time, when it's better to hit singles and doubles.

So your initial reaction to the trading losses was to swing for home runs, trying to catch up, and that effort nearly broke you. Yet these strikeouts clearly taught you a lesson. How did you claw your way back?

Other traders told me, "Don't think about the money; think about trading. Just try to make $500 a day." So I just tried to book profits. By booking profits, the big numbers come eventually. Five hundred dollars a day is 10 grand a month. Then I would try to make $1000 a day. That's $20,000 a month. Three months later I had made all my money back. *From this, I realized the importance of getting out of a trade when you can, not when you have to. Nobody ever went poor from taking profits.* It's a lot worse when a half-dollar profit in a stock turns into a loser.

When you've lost tens of thousands of dollars and you try to make it back on $500 a day, the uphill trudge can seem endless. At that pace, with roughly 20 trading days a month, you would have to endure months of hard work just to break even.

When you are down that kind of money and you make $500, you feel, "Big deal, I didn't even make a dent." But if you have a mentality of "I must book profits," the next thing you know, your profits get bigger and bigger.

It makes sense to think smaller, in both dollars and number of shares at risk. But it's worth noting that you refer to booking profits as a mental process—a kind of psychological cheerleading. What would you say is the dominant mind-set that put you on the right track?

It's confidence. When you're losing money every day and you're finally down $53,000, you have no confidence left. You're thinking, what am I going to do now that I'm down so much money? There is no way that you believe you can still trade. Then you come in for a week, Monday through Friday, and you make $300, $500, $800. You think, I made money five days in a row. I can definitely do this. And then you build up the confidence to say, "I'm just going to make a few hundred dollars a day."

Some people are down to their last chip and they sulk away, completely beaten. Others—and perhaps this is true of traders—get a perverse thrill from having nowhere to go but up. But regaining confidence requires a lot of work; it's not as easy as rolling the dice.

I saw people around my office making money and I would think, they're not smarter than I am. I follow the market, I see the stocks; why can't I do this? Then I started picking their brains. I'd be here until 5:30 P.M., long after the market closed and everyone is out of here. I'd stick around and look over their trades for the day. I saw, for example, that I bought Intel and so did they. Where did they buy? Where did I buy? If they bought lower and I bought higher, I knew I wasn't buying at the right time. I should have bought when they did.

It's back to the old rule: know where stocks are coming from. When I looked over someone else's trades and saw that they bought a stock ⅜ of a point cheaper than I did, I realized that I wasn't really following this stock like I should be.

When you talk about confidence, you're actually describing two types—and you've experienced them both. On one hand is the confidence that brought you back from that punishing initial loss. Then there's the confidence you had the first time you sat down to trade. That naïvete was

quickly blown away, but in its place you seem to have built a stronger framework.

The market can humble you quickly. As confident as I was when I came in, a month later I was very humble as far as trading goes. It is different now. I'm confident that I am a good trader. When I started, I was confident that I would be a good trader. I had no idea whether I could be a good trader or not. I just figured I'd be good because I've been good at things my whole life. You think no one can beat you when you first start trading. But really it's not an easy job at all.

You claim you're a good trader. How about some more tips? What kind of market condition or stock characteristics do you like to see before you trade?

I'm a firm believer in relative strength and relative weakness. The Dow is down 50 points, NASDAQ's down big, and everything looks awful, yet here's a stock—say Amgen—that's up a quarter. So everything is getting whacked—Microsoft, Intel, Cisco, they're all down—and here is a stock that is up on the day. As soon as the market starts looking up, that's the first stock I am going to buy. Or suppose the market is really strong and everything is up big. But here's a stock that's down a quarter. When the market sells off, that stock is the first one I'm going short. *I always have a game plan.*

Your having a game plan isn't surprising. Even though it appears chaotic, electronic day trading involves a tremendous amount of foresight. Winning day traders always are looking ahead to the next move. Does strategy and planning come naturally to you?

I've always been a street-smart person, always logical.

"Street-smart" seems more of a gut response. Are street smarts important to being a successful trader?

Street smart is so much more important than book smart. You can take any Ivy League guy who is 4.0 out of Harvard, but if he isn't street smart in logic and quick thinking, he's not going to make money in this job.

How then would you define "street-smart"?

For me, it's being quick on your feet. A lot of people look at stocks and think, should I buy it? They tend to overanalyze. There's no time for that. I do momentum trading. If the stock has momentum going up, I'm going to buy it, ride it for a profit, and sell it. I see a stock going up, I hit it up, boom, buy, and the next thing you know I own a few thousand shares of that stock.

Where did you grow up?

Rockland County, New York.

That's not exactly the mean streets of Manhattan. So how did you get into stock trading?

I was working with my dad in the life insurance business. I always wanted to be on Wall Street, ever since I saw the movie *Wall Street*. But I didn't want to be a stockbroker. I didn't want to be sitting on the phone for 14 hours a day, calling people for money. I wanted to be a trader, to be in the action.

Who was your favorite character in *Wall Street*?

Oh, [Gordon] Gekko, no question about that.

Gekko? He was that reptilian character who uttered the infamous line, "Greed is good."

Greed is good.

Do you believe that?

To a point. It can get out of hand.

I recall that Gordon Gekko got his comeuppance in the end.

Yeah, he did. I wanted to be Gordon Gekko up to a point. I think greed is good until you start screwing over whoever you have to. That part is not good.

It's true that greed can be a great motivator. But greed also can spur a trader to act hastily, and as you've pointed out, it's critical to watch the action, size up the situation, and then make your move. Would you say that sticking to a game plan requires patience, discipline, or both?

I don't think patience is really important to being a good trader. You can be patient and wait for what you want, but it still won't happen. Discipline is saying, *"I'm wrong, I'm getting out of the stock and actually doing it."* Sometimes you'll be long in a stock and all of a sudden it's falling. Undisciplined people get stubborn and say, "It's going to go up," or "It's going down, I'll buy more and eventually it will go back up." *The discipline to admit when you are wrong, get out, and not take a big loss is what makes a great trader.*

You also spoke about the importance of selling a stock when you can, not when you have to. At the moment of such a decision, what is your screen telling you to do?

When a stock's going up and you're long, you want to sell into upward momentum. *In other words, sell when you can, not when you have to.* Or suppose you're long in a stock and the market is acting great, but your stock's not going up. When it starts ticking down, get out. Because the next thing you know, buyers dry up and the stock comes down harder. If I'm long a stock and I'm selling on the way up, who cares how much higher it goes? I sold when I could—on the way up. I booked a profit. I'm thrilled.

How do you choose a stock? Do you scan the newspapers for stories and use that information to form an opinion?

About three months after I first started, I was reading an article in *The Wall Street Journal* about some analyst or money manager who was negative on semiconductor stocks. I came in to work with the opinion that semiconductors were weak. So I shorted Intel and all these semiconductor makers. "Opposite" isn't even the word to describe what happened that day. Every semiconductor stock was up—they exploded. Since that day, the only reading I do in the morning is the [New York] *Daily News* sports section. I have not read a financial newspaper in two years. I will put on CNBC just to get a feel for where the market is going to open and what stocks might be hot. But I really don't want to have any opinions before I get to work. I want to come in, 9:30 A.M. the market opens, and read the tape. *Let the market tell me where it's going to go, not a newspaper.*

"Reading the tape" refers to the old-fashioned ticker tape that used to print out every stock trade. Speculators would study the prints, and the combination of share volume and price would signal whether money was flowing into or out of a stock. Famed trader Jesse Livermore made—and lost—a fortune in this way. Today, the "tape" is electronic. So how exactly do you "read" it?

Reading the tape is watching stocks and their levels. Where is a stock going? Where is it coming from? If a stock is going up, what level won't it go through? The next time it goes up again and hits that level, I want to short it. But if it breaks through, I'm wrong. Then I want to go long because it went through a level it couldn't before.

You don't ask questions?

Oh, no. I don't care why it did it. All I know is that it broke through the level. Here is a stock that tried several times to get through a level and couldn't. Then it succeeds. It's probably a long now.

A stock cracks one level and you cover the short and go long. That makes sense, but what if the breakout is a false start?

It could be.

Don't you want to be sure?

Again, you're talking levels. Say a stock breaks resistance at $31⅞. How high should I let it go? $32? $32⅛? Do I want to pay $32⅛? Then the people who have bought at ¾ are selling to me. That's like when I first started trading and I used to buy Intel when it was all the way up. Except then I didn't know where Intel was coming from. Now I know. Why should I pay $32⅛ if I can buy for $31⅞? The stock just broke through major resistance. It should go higher. If it doesn't, I was wrong, I'm out, I take my losses.

The beauty of watching and knowing levels is that you're simultaneously developing a picture of a stock's overhead

resistance—the selling pressure—and downside support, or buying pressure. What's an example of a trade where reading the tape and knowing levels worked to your advantage?

Today I had 10,000 shares of Netscape short. I made $1.25 on it. The stock opened up 2½ points on earnings news. The market overall was acting great all morning. Then I watched Netscape pull in a dollar. Now here's stock that makes good earnings, up $2½, and it just pulled in $1. That's quite a big sell-off.

So much for the power of positive thinking. From your seat, you can almost feel the selling pressure build.

Exactly. The market started going higher, but Netscape rallied maybe just another quarter. So I realize it's not a strong stock anymore, and I started shorting it.

Once you got short Netscape, what happened? How did the trade play out?

I shorted a few thousand at $32¼. The stock went down to $31½, up only ½ now on the day. Then it started rallying. I held my short. I wanted to see how far it would rally. It went back up to $31⅞, which is a lower high from where I shorted. Now I could see it was making lower highs and lower lows. If the market starts pulling in, this stock is the first one going down. So I started shorting some more. Next thing you know I'm short 10,000. I made $12,000 in about 12 minutes and then covered the short ⅛ off the low for the day. It was a perfect trade. I had my game plan figured out. I knew what I was going to do. I executed it perfectly, where I shorted it and where I covered.

On this day you went home a hero. There also are times when you don't want to show your face at the front door. Talk about a trade that fell apart on you.

A few days before the Netscape trade, I was short a computer chip stock called Rambus. The stock came in, rallied, but made lower lows and lower highs. So I stayed short. Then the market starts to rally, and the stock didn't do anything. I'm thinking, hey, Rambus is still weak. The market pulls back in—and then it explodes. It just rips, and Rambus goes with it. When you are short a few thousand shares and stocks are ripping, everyone is trying to buy. I'm not going to be first to get filled. I lost a point and a half on 6000 shares, and it hurt.

How did you react once you finally covered the short? You've just lost $9000. Did you call it a day, or try to get whole?

I was down $9000 and decided to keep trading. I said to myself, let me just get down $7000 and I'll be happy. Then it was, let's see if I can just get down $5000. I was setting small goals, trying to make a quarter here, a quarter there, fighting my way back. I wound up losing $4000 on the day, and if I go home down $4000, it's a lot better than going home down $9000.

What is most striking about these experiences is that you got burned on Rambus in a big way, then copied that same strategy to trade Netscape. Weren't you afraid of being hit with another huge loss?

I trade the same way every day.

When you lose a chunk of money, won't you review the bad trade and consider changing your tactics?

I believe in relative strength, relative weakness, knowing your levels, and seeing how the stock reacts to the rest of the market. If I'm wrong one day, that doesn't mean that suddenly my strategies are wrong. Rambus just ripped up. If I see a stock that's weak compared to the whole market, I'm going to short that stock. I got burned—I was wrong—but I still think I did the right thing.

It takes courage or stubbornness—maybe both—to be wrong about a trade but still believe you made the right decision.

If Intel is up ½ on the day when Microsoft, Cisco, and Dell Computer are down $2 to $3, I know that when the market turns up, Intel is the first stock to buy because it's relatively strong to the rest of the market. If Intel ends up dropping and I lose money on the trade, I still think I did the right thing. That was the right game plan to have. Relative to the market, Intel was the strongest stock. If it didn't work, it didn't work, but it's the right trade to do.

The market called you wrong, and yet you didn't yield. If that's how the game is played, why are traders in awe of the all-powerful, all-seeing market?

The market does humble you and tell you what to do. But more times than not, I'll be right. In a relative strength and relative weakness strategy, there's a reason why Intel is up ½ when the market is tanking. There are buyers in the stock. If Goldman Sachs and Merrill Lynch and First Boston are bidding Intel up, I'm not going against these guys and thinking it's a short. They are holding the stock up. It's up ½ when the market is weak. That stock is strong. When the market starts going up, you would think that Intel is the first to lead. So even if I lose money in the trade, I still did right buying that stock.

It's probably fair to say you don't lose sleep over a missed opportunity.

No, I don't. I might say, "I could have made money in the stock. I had it, I knew it, but I missed it." I'm not going to go crazy. I'm not the kind of guy who breaks keyboards and curses. What am I going to do? Move on.

Will you look at the same stock later in the day and try to buy it at a different level?

Sure. A lot of times people say they made a half a dollar on the trade, and then it went $2 higher. The first thing I say to them is, "Why don't you buy it back?" If you think it's going to rip another half, buy it right back. But if the stock's moved too far already, don't chase it.

If traders have strong convictions about a stock, why don't they just hold their position a bit longer instead of jumping in and out?

I guess they were happy with their half a dollar. Half a point is $500. That's a lot of money to make on a stock. They're thrilled, and move on to the next trade. Whereas I'll watch to see how much higher it goes. That's when I start focusing on levels to see where it stops. *You've got to be 100 percent focused on the levels of the stocks you're trading.* Anything less and you'll never make money.

One of the rewards for knowing your levels is the ability to buy a stock for the bid price instead of at the offer, thereby capturing the market maker's spread. Describe how these two key elements of a trade—the levels and the bid—work together to maximize a day trader's profit.

Say a stock is trading for $30 by $30⅛, and the bid goes up to $30½, comes back to $30, goes up to $30¾, and comes back to $30. You're getting a feel for the swings. At $30, I'm going to bid. If it goes up ½, I'm going to sell. Now maybe some guy paid $30¼ and feels the stock is going down. He's going to try to sell at $30, take his ¼ loss, and get out. There I am bidding $30. So I am buying into the downward momentum, but I'm also getting a feel for the support levels. Let's say I'm wrong and it goes to $29⅞. I'm only losing ⅛. If I initially paid the offer, $30⅛, I'd be risking at least ¼ to see if it held support.

Also, I am going to buy at a level where there is support. If I see 10 market makers bidding $30 and the stock is falling down, I'm going to bid $30 1/16. Whoever wants to sell is going to sell to me first. If I think it's going to keep going down—remember there were 10 market makers bidding $30—I'll sell it to one of those guys at $30. So I lost 1/16. I'm going to trade at a level where I see support from other market makers. If I'm wrong, I'm out and I don't lose much money. If I am right, I have a stock on the bid instead of the offer.

Day trading, especially with a momentum strategy, is becoming increasingly popular. This ultra-short-term approach to the market clearly has momentum of its own. How about you? Will you still be day trading five years from now?

I hope so. I can honestly say that I'm the only one of my friends who can't wait to get to work. Sunday night, when my friends are upset that tomorrow morning is work, I can't sleep because I'm so excited.

Are you excited to get to work even when you're down a few grand?

I have down days—I don't have down months.

Marc McCord
Control Emotions

---

*"Great traders look at the market and make logical,
unemotional decisions."*

M arc McCord was raised in working-class Bayside,
Queens, several miles and many worlds away from Wall
Street. For him, the trading bug bit early. While most of his
high school classmates were grappling with the cost of a Sat-
urday night date, McCord used $3500 saved from a newspaper
delivery route to speculate on the price of copper and gold.

That bet ended badly. McCord lost all of his money, but he
was hooked. He set out to learn more about trading and to
become better at it. When his high school economics teacher
noticed McCord studying market research on gold and silver,
he taught him key aspects of technical analysis and stock
charting that McCord uses still.

The hits started to come. By his early 20s, McCord was
trading commodity options with money from a handful of
retail clients as working capital. Shrewd trades in gold and
other markets helped turn $180,000 into $1.7 million, he

recalls. The view looked pretty sweet from that lofty perch. Then came October 1987 and the stock market crash. McCord and his clients were caught on the wrong side of the fence. In one crushing blow, the entire portfolio was wiped out.

Chagrined, McCord vowed not to handle retail accounts again. He became a floor trader at the American Stock Exchange, buying and selling stock options in his own account. Six years later, McCord left the Exchange for the lure of electronic day trading.

McCord is a quick-witted 34-year-old with a streetwise edge who doesn't need much prompting to rattle off a stream of urgent, highly charged trading tips. Over the years and through many ups and downs, he has built up a tight set of these hard-and-fast rules. The biggest: controlling emotions. That's odd advice from someone whose talk and actions practically scream emotion. *But keeping emotions and ego in check, he claims, is the most important secret of successful traders.* Easier said than done.

■   ■   ■

You became involved in commodities trading while still in high school. What's a 15-year-old doing in the highly speculative commodities market?

A friend of my older brother got involved with a commodity company. He called my brother and got me on the phone. I decided to invest some money—my whole life savings—which I lost in about a week.

All from one phone call. How much did you lose?

About $3500.

That's a lot of money to drop anytime, let alone in a week.

Especially when you're flinging papers around Bayside, Queens, for years to save up that kind of money, and then blow it in a week speculating in something you know nothing about.

But the trading bug obviously had bit you hard. Have there been other times in your career when defeat has been snatched from the jaws of victory?

I traded commodity options in the mid-1980s. I had turned $180,000 into close to $1.7 million and lost it all on the day of the crash in October 1987.

You lost $1.7 million in a day?

Lost it all. I was managing a small portfolio for retail clients, and basically I turned $180,000 into $1.7 million and then lost it all. And then I realized that I didn't want to do retail. When you lose $1.7 million and you have to call up Mr. Jones and Mrs. Jones and say, "Listen, you know you sent me $15,000 and I turned it into $40,000? Well now you owe me $10,000 to close your account." When you make 20 of those phone calls, you realize that you don't want to be in the retail business anymore. After that, I got my way down to the floor of the American Stock Exchange, trading stock options for myself.

It's always the unexpected punch that knocks you flat. Then it feels like you'll never get up.

And I was young, in my early 20s.

And you lost your own money as well.

I had a lot of my own money in there and blew that, too.

What did you learn from this experience?

Never listen to anyone.

So now you trade for yourself alone. It's your gut feeling, and if you make a mistake, it's your pain.

I go with my own instinct. And I know that if everyone says something is going to happen—it's definitely wrong.

Going against the herd is a widely prescribed conventional wisdom. Don't fight the tape is another. But these two pieces of advice are contradictory. How do successful traders know when to move boldly and when to fight another day?

You have to control your emotions at all times. Good, bad, indifferent—you have to be even keel. You can't let the market get to you. Second, *the market is never wrong.* You're either right with the market or wrong with the market. People sit there and bang their chest, "I'm right; the market's wrong." You're kidding me. You can be a bit faster than everyone else and try to get out of a position before them or enter a trade before them, but don't think you're going to beat them. If it's going up, buy it. If they're going down, sell with them.

The most important advice you would give a new trader is to control emotions?

And then the rest will come.

Everyone's a genius in a bull market, but the market does have ways of rudely reminding us who's boss. Accordingly, investors and traders do need to handle emotions. Whether you feel on top of the world or on the bottom, it helps to

know that reality is somewhere in between. But a reality check—that self-restraint—doesn't come easily.

It's very hard to do, but you just have to leave your ego behind. Emotions and ego are very similar things in trading. Someone with a small ego can be up or down a lot of money, and you look at him and you'll never know. A good poker player never shows his hand. A guy with an ego has to raise the bet or bet the limit. He'll bet the other players right out of the hand. If he didn't have ego and was smart, he would show no emotion. He would bet a little bit and get everybody to play with him—and then smoke 'em. In that regard, I would guess that attorneys who become traders do well.

Why would an attorney make a good trader?

Because they think logically on their feet. They see through all the noise. They could be right in front of the jury and not let any of their surroundings bother them. They just see what they have to do. They are very focused; they know what their job is. They probably trade similarly. *Great traders look at the market and make logical, unemotional decisions.*

What you're suggesting is that successful trading demands the kind of linear thinking that a legal mind might possess.

Right. Sometimes what is, isn't, and what isn't, is. And lawyers can really see that because they are trained to rely on fact rather than be deceived by what someone might want them to believe.

Is truth a rare commodity in day trading?

Absolutely. What is, isn't and what isn't, is. The best advice I ever read in *Market Wizards* is when Paul Tudor Jones says, "Don't focus on making money; focus on protecting what you have." And when I trade that way, I make money. I was raised in a rough neighborhood in Queens, New York, and I was taught that the best defense is a strong offense. In trading, it's the complete opposite. *When you are constantly going on the offensive and thinking only about making money and the profit in the trade—never looking at the downside—you're going to get beat.*

"Downside" is just a polite term for losing money. And day traders make the job look effortless—fortunes are a keystroke away. Nothing could be more false. For as you say, a big part of success is controlling risk—the amount you can lose on a trade. What strategies do you use to minimize risk and maximize gains?

Know where the stock is coming from. That means know where the stock has been. Have some idea where it's traded—yesterday, today, the hour, or the minute. Anytime I jump into a stock where I just buy or sell based upon movement of that stock, 85 percent of those traders are losers. I might get lucky 15 percent of the time. When I lose I get mad and I'm like, I did it again. It ruins my whole day. It's so stupid. Would I ever just take a $100 bill, with a $20 and a $5 and take a match to it?

Trading is surreal in that way. Since you're not tangibly holding the cash, it can lose some of its meaning.

Right, and you just say, "My God, what are you doing?" You just blew 125 bucks, or five hundred, or a thousand, two thousand dollars. Twenty $100 bills you just took a lighter to. Are you kidding me?

A $1000 here, $2000 there, and pretty soon you're talking about real money.

It gets to you. Mistakes like that probably cost me $100,000 a year in losses. So don't buy stock when you don't know where it's coming from and you don't know what it's doing. *Take profits when you can, not when you have to.* When a trade is in your favor, take profits. At a minimum, sell half. When a trade turns against you, you're not better than the market—just get out. Simple stuff. But you know what? Nobody follows it. Including me.

That's hard to believe. Clearly, you follow your advice more often than not. The crucial reason to know where a stock is coming from is to give a hint of where it might go. To do that, you have to be aware of its support and resistance levels; you have to know its strengths and weaknesses.

More than that, you have to remember things like Amazon.com went to $132 a share six weeks ago and failed there, and now Deutsche Morgan Grenfell's market maker is offering at $132, and you know that DMGL helped bring Amazon public. The stock is trading 131¾, and you're selling if DMGL is on the offer at $132. A good trader remembers all of these stupid numbers and all of these crazy stocks. That's what it's all about. I personally follow 140 stocks. A beginning trader should only follow two to five stocks. And they should trade 100 shares, not 1000. And they should never pay the spread. They need to learn to think like the market maker. Before I buy any stock, I follow it, I watch it, and then I bid for it.

Day trading has a "keyboard cowboy" reputation, but you're actually saying that the job requires tremendous patience.

Right. You have to sit and watch. I do a lot of saltwater fly-fishing. And before I fish, I watch them feed. What do the fish like that make them come up and feed? The guy just throwing the line back and forth doesn't know what's really going on. But if you know the feeding frenzy and you know the feeding pattern, the rest is just getting the line in the water.

Describe a trade where both patience and knowing how a stock is moving made all the difference.

Today, for example, Morgan Stanley was the seller at Amazon.com. He was a big buyer yesterday at 107⅞. But today, Morgan Stanley was the seller at $111. The market—the Standard and Poor's 500 Index futures—is coming in, meaning it's going lower, and you're looking to short Amazon. The disciplined trader will try to sell it on the offer with Morgan Stanley, knowing he can lean on him and buy it back to get out if the market or the Internets turn around. An emotional person, seeing the market fall apart, will hit a bid if it's an uptick, trying to get short, not even seeing if Morgan Stanley is on the offer. The only time I was looking to short Amazon is if Morgan was on the offer and I was trying to sell stock with him. I might also teenie him—if he was selling at 11⅛ I would offer stock at 11¹⁄₁₆. If the market is now 10¾ or 11⅛, I'm capturing the spread and leaning on the seller.

What do you mean by "leaning on the seller"?

When you lean on something, you know it has support. If you lean on a wall, you know that the wall is going to catch you. If you lean on water, you're going to fall in. I know that

Morgan is a seller at, say, 11⅛. So if I were to short 11⅛ stock
and market conditions were to change where I felt the market
was going higher, I could buy stock back from him to get out
of the position. I'm leaning on his sell order, trying to get a free
look on the downside. It's a free look because I know that I can
get out from Morgan.

What can go wrong in this situation?

Morgan flips from the offer to the bid—becomes a
buyer—and you could be in trouble. You're going to lose $750
to $1000 unless you're a very shrewd trader. Everything can go
numb. Morgan's sell order—or seller—is gone. Buyers
reemerge. Traders who are short have to cover and new guys
want to get long. Now you'll have all this buying pressure. An
unemotional, disciplined, risk-averse trader will sell on the
offer with Morgan or move ⅟₁₆ below, will not hit the bid, and
will always be aware of where Morgan Stanley is. Because,
bottom line, he is what we call the ax.

The ax?

He's the man that can move the stock. He is working a
large order or taking a stance.

He's the executioner.

Right. So we call him the ax. He's the man in that stock
for that day. Tomorrow he might not even be there. But today,
the seller to lean on was Morgan Stanley.

**Leaning on a seller involves what you were saying earlier
about the best offense being a strong defense. What are
some other defensive tactics you use?**

When you're in the trade, here are my rules. If you're a novice, never let a trade go more than a quarter against you. No matter what, have a line in the sand that says if I buy Microsoft at 102 and it goes to 101¾, I'm out. I'm not going down to $101½ and hoping. *Ask yourself what you are willing to risk in any trade and stick to it.*

Second, *never let a profit turn into a loss.* Say you have ⅞ of a dollar profit. If it goes to ⅝, I'll get out. Similarly, if you're up half a dollar on a 1000-share trade, you have $500 in your back pocket. If you let it turn into a $500 loss, that's burning ten $100 bills. Suppose a stock went from $36 to $35½. You think that if it goes back to $36, it has to fall back to $35½. Are you kidding? The whole perception of the stock has changed. Maybe a buyer has come into the market, the market has gotten better, or another stock in the sector has gotten better. The sun came out. Who knows? *Remember, the market knows all. The market is never wrong.*

How do you prepare yourself for the trading day?

The first thing I do is look at stock charts. I've day traded S&P 500 futures; I've day traded gold; I did options on the floor of the American Stock Exchange. I ran a futures desk for a large commodities company, and I've always relied on one thing: a simple, daily bar chart. That's it. A daily high and a daily low for the past three to six months. That's all I need. I just want to see formation, top, bottom, support, resistance. Charts tell me where a stock has been and also give a good feel of where it's going.

With charting, you literally have to read between the lines. What are you hoping to find?

Sector sympathy and what I call the Domino Effect. If Yahoo! is strong or has news, for instance, I immediately look at the other stocks in the Internet sector. I don't need to go where everyone is. The masses lose their asses. So I'll look at Amazon, Lycos, Excite, and CMG Information Services, which is an Internet holding company. That's my game. I take all these charts and overlay them, trying to find divergence. And if I find something that has not gone with the group, I'll start concentrating on it. When the semiconductors are hot, I do the same thing with Novell, Applied Materials, Lam Research. Technical analysis gives me a feel for the whole sector, which might give me an opinion for the day or for the week.

So before the market opens, you chart the stocks that interest you for the day, looking for divergent patterns. Then 9:30 A.M. comes and the opening bell is rung. What's your move?

I look to see how the market reacts. There is usually a gap in the morning. Does the gap hold? If I find that a stock is strong, I'll let the opening go through, let them clean up the marginal orders, and then wait for the stock to come in a little bit. I'm watching how the Standard & Poor's 500 is acting, and how the leaders like Yahoo!, Amazon, Dell, Intel, and Microsoft are acting. Because a lot of times the opening is nothing but a lying farce. Market makers take these stocks to levels where they shouldn't be in the first place.

As you've said, day trading involves a keen sense of timing. What tools do you use to determine when to step on the gas and make a trade?

I follow a one-minute bar chart for the S&P 500, the NAS-DAQ futures, and U.S. Treasury bonds; together they give a feel for the direction of the overall market. I keep stock charts in my head. A stock in an uptrend will make higher lows and higher highs during the trading day. The correct time to bid is when the stock is making a higher low. I bid into a pullback of a stock that is in an uptrend. If I buy it on the bid I am able to save the spread as opposed to paying it, and if I buy it on a pullback I am again minimizing my risk by limiting my downside. If it holds the higher low I'm potentially a big winner. If it fails and makes a new low I take a small loss.

How frequently can you pull this off in a given day?

Two or three times in any one stock. And that's where I get to a theory called "dancing the dance." You've got to know other stocks. It's like the sock hops with the girls on one side of the room and the guys on the other. If you make that ⅝ in a stock, it's tempting to keep dancing with it. But you've got to give the others a shot. On the flip side, if you lose ¼, don't go back. I see a lot of novices who lose a quarter and then lose 10 more quarters in a row in the same stock, making the same mistakes, when there are 50 other beautiful stocks to dance with.

Of course, this trading dance demands some fancy foot-work. One of the hot steps is to pocket the spread—buying on the bid or selling on the offer. How does this strategy play out?

Say Microsoft is trading $105 at $105⅛. Microsoft is a large-cap stock with a huge volume and narrow spreads. Big stocks like Microsoft, Dell, Intel, Cisco Systems, 3Com, all have narrow spreads—anywhere from a teenie—¹⁄₁₆—to ⅛.

Now if a $105 bid has Goldman, Morgan Stanley, Paine Webber, and Smith Barney on its side, and the planets are in line, meaning the Dow Jones is up, the S&P 500 is up, bonds are doing what they should be doing, as well as the NASDAQ, you have what I call convergence in the market. I am going to bid with these market makers. I'm not going to buy 1000 shares of Microsoft at ⅛ on the offer. As soon as you put that position on, you are down $125. I'm going to try to buy on the $105 bid along with the big market players.

What if no market maker or trader will hit your bid?

If you're bidding $105 for 30 seconds and you can't get a hit, then you might want to move to $105¹⁄₁₆ and go high bid for the stock. Now you have only a $62.50 risk on 1000 shares.

There are also those pitches that are hit right off the bat—and then the market maker moves the bid to the next level down.

If you get hit on the bid immediately and the bid drops below you—Goldman, Morgan, Paine Webber start dropping their bids—you know that you are in trouble. You want to try to sell as quickly as possible.

What about trades you don't want to exit quickly? I would imagine that sometimes the picture looks so good that you just want to keep staring at it. Or does that go against day-trading dogma?

No. When a stock is going your way, you've got to sit on your hands. You've got 'em. There's no reason to give it away. The thing to do then is to let it ride, but you have to be careful not to let a winner turn into a loser. "If I've got ⅞ profit, I'm not going to let it go to less than ⅝. If I had $6, I'd say to myself, "I'm taking $5 out of this trade." If it's up $7, I'll take $6 out. *You've got to be quick to take losses and slow to take a profit.*

Describe how you handled one of your best trades, where you let profits ride and the wave just rolled along for you.

That happened with Colt Telecom, a British telecommunications company. There were some bullish articles about Colt, and top analysts had the stock as their number one or number two pick. I followed the stock four to five months, saw it break out, and bought 2000 at $146. It went in my favor probably $3. I said I really don't want to sell until it goes to $200. As it happened, I sold a thousand shares up 8 and made $8000, and just let the other one go. That's one of my rules— sell half. Lock it in, ring the cash register. Like I say, *sell it when you can, not when you have to.* And then let the rest ride.

How long did you hold this position?

For about five trading days. I sold the other thousand at about $175. But this was unusual. I don't recommend it unless you are up hundreds of thousands of dollars and you really know that stock. But the trend is your friend. Like I said, when you've got 'em, there's no reason to give it to them.

What do you think are some advantages that electronic day traders have over other stock traders?

An electronic day trader has constant action and constant information coming into his computer. If he concentrates on a sector or a group or a small group of stocks and he's disciplined and selective, there's just so much opportunity. Whereas if you're trading only one stock, every stock has its day. It gets busy and then gets quiet. I can remember when I was a floor trader making a lot of money in Apple Computer options, for instance, and then Apple went sour and things got very tough. We went from a 40-man crowd to a 6-man crowd.

So much liquidity down the drain. That must have made life interesting. How do you trade a wallflower stock versus a beauty queen with many bidders and a lot of action?
Very carefully.

What do you mean, "very carefully"?
You've got to be very careful what you do in the 6-man crowd. There's a forgiving rim and a nonforgiving rim. When there's a 40-man crowd and you make a mistake on a 10 lot (1000 shares), you're probably going to get out right away for ⅛ and lock in the loss. In a 6-man crowd, they know you screwed up—but they're not going to let you out.

The market makers will let you out—but you'll have to fork over your wallet first.
Right. If there's a 40-man crowd and 4 people around you know you just messed up, but 35 guys on the other side of the crowd have no idea. They're not going to know what your position is; they're not going to know what's going on. The 6-man crowd will know exactly what you just did. It's just like trading Intel versus an illiquid stock. Intel trades millions of shares a day and you know that you can cover your mistakes for a small loss. But in smaller, illiquid stocks, both the wide spreads and lack of volume will make your mistakes much more costly.

So you lose your anonymity in a small crowd?

There is nowhere to hide.

Day traders then are better off in stocks that have larger groups of market makers?

Where do you think I'm better off? Microsoft, trading 15 million shares a day, or Colt Telcom that trades 25,000 shares a day? Where is the depth and liquidity? Where's the out? The out is in Microsoft. You buy 3000 Microsoft and lose a teenie on it in two seconds and feel no pain. You buy 3000 Colt Telecom, you might not have an out for $10. It's risk versus reward.

It occurs to me that the sectors and stocks you trade might have a seasonality to them. Do certain industries perform better at different times of the year?

Absolutely. In winter, the oil sector will get hot, depending on supply and demand for crude oil. So the drillers will act well or poorly based on the climate. After Christmas you'll see how the retailers did. I'll start trading Nordstrom, Bed Bath & Beyond, maybe some other retailers based upon how Christmas shopping went. There's a domino effect on computer sales, so I watch how CompUSA is doing, which will then impact Dell, CDW Computer. If they're selling personal computers, people will eventually get online.

Are there any predictable trading trends to watch for during spring and summer?

In summer, companies report by the latter part of August. Then you start getting a September rally because everyone comes back from vacation in the Hamptons and all that farce. September through November is usually very good and hot in biotech. I'm not certain why. I think the Food and Drug Administration makes many patent approval decisions at that time of the year. Some smart trader once told me that September, October, and November are when you want to look at the biotechs and pharmaceutical companies. But there is always something going on. In the summer of 1997, the semiconductors were hot. In the spring of 1998, it was the Internet explosion. How many stocks do we have on NASDAQ? Thousands. There is always a stock in play. The stock market is nothing but a huge menu of opportunities.

Sure, you can make a lot of dough from day trading. But as you well know, you also can lose plenty. Why do you do it?

Because I love action. Always have, always will. I love to trade. And it doesn't matter if it's a box of rusty nails, if it's copper, if it's Apple Computer options, if it's cocoa, or if it's Amazon.com. I have to trade. Electronic trading has completely changed my life—to nothing but the better. I can do it from my house, from an airplane, from a hotel room, or with a group of people who are 20 sets of eyes following 20 sets of stocks.

Many people are going to ignore your pragmatic advice. They'll focus on the action, the chase—the juice that keeps you going. They think they'll know when to go long and when to short, and that the intricacies of electronic trading will come easily and quickly to them.

That attitude will really bring the lamb to slaughter. A person who says, "I know there is going to be an initiation and I'm going to lose money at the beginning. Now I'm not going to lose $35,000, but I'm willing to lose $3500 to understand the mechanics of the system and the mechanics of the market."

Those guys are going to do okay. But the people who say, "I'm going to rip 'em up and make $5000 a day"—who think day trading is so easy—those are the people I want to trade with, because I'm just going to take their money day in and day out. This market is a zero-sum game. If there's a buyer, there's a seller. If there's a winner, there's a loser.

Perhaps you can recall what happened when you first started to day trade?

I paid a lot of spreads; I didn't follow my levels and would let a profitable day go negative. When you achieve a goal of $3000 a day, you have to walk away. And that's hard for me. But you've got to take those chips, put them in your pocket, walk up to the cashier, and leave.

What do you think the future holds for day traders? Will we look back and say that the chance to make and lose fortunes via computer was just a brief flash in the pan?

I have two dear friends—one made $3 million trading commodities last year. And he's ready to leave the floor and come do this with me. My other friend is a partner at a major brokerage firm who hates what I do for a living, hates talking to me about it, and thinks that we will not be here in two years. He thinks I should close up my shop and go back to the stock exchange floor.

There's a resounding vote of confidence. Coming from a good friend, how do you reply?

I believe he is 100 percent wrong. Electronic day trading—as well as electronic trading—is going to grow at a rapid pace. The New York Stock Exchange might be in for a rude awakening. I think one day all markets worldwide will be nothing but electronic. Human beings will not be there for open outcry markets.

Sell exchange seats short.

You got it.

You've been around trading pits and markets for more than half of your life. What leads you to be so bullish on electronic trading?

The Internet is growing and growing—it's crazy. Eventually almost everyone who buys a computer is going to be online. Anyone who's got risk capital will eventually trade stocks through on online service. Not that they're going to leave their professions, but it will bring electronic trading to a higher level.

So realistically, how much money do you need to start day trading?

At the beginning—to learn—you need at least $25,000, with the intention of coming up with another $50,000. Buying power is the key. If you have $50,000, for instance, you have a two-to-one margin and can buy $100,000 worth of stock. I like to trade with at least $300,000 cash in my account, giving me $600,000 buying power. So that I know that I can buy 4000 Microsoft, 1000 Yahoo, and 1000 Amazon and not worry about it.

You also need a piped-in system that's going to supply Level 2 quotes that give you parity with the NASDAQ market makers. Simply placing an order with an online brokerage doesn't quite cut it.

That's a different story. I believe at that point you are an investor. I am a professional day trader. Professional traders are tick traders—they know every tick in their stock. And they try to buy the first tick and make ⅟₁₆ or ⅛. And these guys can make thousands of dollars a day doing it.

You are making a distinction between a trader and an investor?

Absolutely. The guy who's calling a broker is more of an investor in today's trading arena.

Even if he's in a stock for just a day?

Yep.

Why is a brokerage customer so different from you?

He doesn't know what's really going on. He's not seeing the whole picture. He probably doesn't have access to detailed quotes (Level 2) or up-to-the-second breaking news.

I'm curious about one final aspect of your work. Every weekday you buy and sell tens of thousands of shares of stock. Where do you invest your money?

Cash. I've been broke too many times. I did it once at the age of 21, and once at 29. I'm not doing it again. Three strikes and you're out. So we're just putting it away. We have some aggressive mutual funds for the kids, but everything else is cash.

Steve Girden
Be Disciplined

"Market makers want day traders to perceive they're something they're not. For day traders, the stock market amounts to one big poker game."

S teve Girden is one of the older players in the electronic day-trading game—a 37-year-old going keyboard to keyboard against a field of mostly twenty-somethings. But he maintains an evenhanded approach and measured tone that reflects nearly a decade of experience as a risk arbitrageur with Wall Street brokerage Bear Stearns.

Risk arbitrageurs, or "arbs," as they're typically called, try to profit from the premium price of corporate takeover plays. These traders will go long the stock of the target company and ride its upward move. At the same time, they sell short the stock of the acquiring company in the expectation that its share price will drop. If all goes to plan, they make money on both the long and short end of the trade. But if the deal collapses, arbs are left holding the bag. Clearly, this is not a business for the fainthearted or the uninformed.

Girden is neither. In fact, he says, the constant pressure is a main attraction of his work. He's also among a minority of day traders who actually pay attention to the opinions and information that newspapers and market pundits deliver each day. Girden reads several newspapers every morning, searching for major and minor chords that can alter the tone of a stock, a sector, or a market. He's what's known as a *bull trader*—looking for big upward market movements that he can climb aboard, or a thread of positive news about a specific company that traders and investors will weave into a higher-priced stock.

The secret to day-trading success, Girden contends, is discipline. And to be sure, being disciplined in a trade or in an approach to the market is also the commandment that's broken most often. Like the other rules of day trading, discipline is easier to talk about than to have. *But everyone knows one truth about discipline: traders who have it the least lose the most.*

■   ■   ■

Day trading seems like a job that's big on control. I hear so often from traders about the importance of controlling risk and controlling losses. I also hear them lament about how difficult this is to achieve. What's so hard about setting limits?

Discipline is—I want to say *was*—my biggest problem. I make a lot and I lose a lot. At first I did not minimize my risks. I used to go for a home run all the time. I'd be up $30,000, down $20,000, up $30,000 again, and down $20,000. I've been trading since I was 22. I was a risk arbitrageur for a major firm and I came to day trading in early 1996, thinking, "Okay, this is going to be simple," and I proceeded to lose a good amount of money very quickly.

Let's be specific. What's a "good amount"?

I was down $60,000 in the first six weeks.

That doesn't sound so good at all. How much did you start with?

I started with $150,000, or $300,000 buying power on margin. So I lost a good percentage of my equity in the beginning. And then I decided to listen to the rules and I proceeded to make $150,000 in the next two months. It was a matter of controlling my losses. I knew I would make money every day, but the real question was how much would I lose? I would make halves or quarters, but I'd lose whole points. That math just doesn't add up. I've gone back and forth over the last 2½ years doing this, where I have great spells and then fall into the same bad habits. But recently I have really made an effort. I'm saying, "Okay, I'm just going to go for singles and doubles." And it's working.

What has changed? Aren't you still the same person you were six months ago?

When I say I'm going to do something—I'm going to take a quarter-point loss—I do it. You don't say, "I'll go another quarter against them." Before you know it, you hit bottom and then you're out of your position. Then it runs up two points and you're saying, "Why did I ever sell?" It's just sticking to the rules. It's easy to make rules, but following the rules is the key here.

That's the point. It's easy to make up rules, but difficult to stick to them. It's really much more comfortable being the rule maker instead of the rule follower.

So you say, "Okay, $1000 is my maximum loss for the day. When I'm down $1000, I'll stop trading." It's hard to carry through that promise. But I'm doing that. Many times I was up a lot of money and gave it all back. But now I have certain limits. If I'm up good money . . .

What is good money to you?

Lately it's been $10,000.

So if you're up $10,000 for the day, then what?

I'll go to lunch, which I never used to do. And I'll put my parameters in place.

What are those rules?

If I give back 20 percent of what I'm up, I can't trade more than three positions. Ordinarily I would trade 10 to 20 positions. And if I give back half of my gains, I trade one position at a time, with no double lots (doubling up). That's the only way to get back your money. You don't want to be up $10,000 and then say, "I want to go for 20 now." That's greed coming into play. It's so hard controlling greed.

So a key to controlling risk in day trading is an ability to temper your greed.

I'm a junkie. I can't see doing anything other than trading stocks. I've been doing it for 16 years and I love it. There is something great about trading something you know all about—stocks like Cisco Systems, Intel, Microsoft, or Dell. I think we are on the tip of the iceberg of technology in the twenty-first century. Just knowing that these companies are leaders and being able to trade them is very exciting to me. But it's easy to get caught up in the madness. I used to follow 500 stocks. About a year ago I got it down to about 300. Now I'm probably down to 100. In the old days I would go home every night with 20 positions. Now it's three or four positions, tops.

Tracking 500 stocks is almost like being a human computer. At the least, that's quite a juggling act. Now you're following 100 names, which is still a plateful. I would guess that the lighter caseload probably allows you to focus better, but wasn't it hard to dump your darlings?

No. I thought it would be. Of course I get upset if I see a stock I used to follow that's up three points. Hopefully somebody else in the room will pick up the stock that you're not seeing. That's the great thing about trading with a group of people. I've thought about opening my own office, but I like the camaraderie. I like having 20 other pairs of eyes around me. I can't see everything anymore. That was my talent. But now there are so many more market makers and so many more people day trading. The market makers having gotten better at this game. And it is a game.

And in this game, there's a steady stream of information and emotion coming at you with lightning speed—what is also called "noise." Now that day trading has become more popular—and you've seen it when it wasn't so—one might assume that the noise has become deafening. How would you describe the changes to day trading over the past couple of years?

You used to watch six things: the S&P 500 futures, the NASDAQ futures, 30-year bond futures, the Dow Jones Industrials, the NASDAQ composite, and the semiconductor, or

SOX, index. It used to be that if the bonds and the S&P futures and the NASDAQ futures are going up, you'd buy Intel, Dell, Microsoft, or Oracle, and you could expect to make a point. It doesn't work that way anymore. There is so much more supply out there, so many more people playing this day-trading game. The spreads have gotten narrower. You used to trade stocks two years ago that were ¾ of a point wide all the time. You play market maker, and you'd definitely take advantage of these spreads.

You'd grab a stock with a ¾-point spread, and then the market maker would lift another ¾, at which point you could cash out with a nice profit.

No question. It used to be called the power uptick. The highflyers were the wide ones. You could pay the spread and make three-quarters of a dollar to a dollar in a second. But it doesn't happen anymore. There just seem to be more supply and more day traders playing the game.

How have narrowing spreads impacted your trading strategy?

Now those stocks, for the most part, are ¹⁄₁₆, ⅛, ¼ of a point wide. It means they're thicker—there's more supply—so it's tougher to break through each level. You get through one level, there's another 20,000 a teenie above. In the old days when you bought the offer at 58¼ there wouldn't be anything until 58¾. The toughest thing I've found is that you can only take out what the market gives you. If your old style worked, and all of a sudden it's not working, it means the market has changed. You have to figure out what to do now to make money.

What do you mean, a trader can only take out what the market gives?

You can't squeeze water out of a stone. If the market is quiet, you can't think, "I'm going to make $10,000 today." There is no volatility. There is no movement. So you can't force the hand. You've got to play slowly, consistently; go for singles and doubles.

There are roughly 20 trading days during the month. Say that on 17 or 18 of those days you play for singles and doubles. Then there might be a triple or a home run on the other days. But if you are looking for the home run every day, you're just going to get caught up in the madness. It's so easy to do when you see all the money being made. Amazon.com moves 20 points in one day and you think, "I should be making more." But if you break it down into the micro rather than the macro viewpoints, all you have to do is make $2000 a day. That's a half-million dollars a year. It's easy to say. I could make $2000 in a flash. But it's staying away from the bad trades that's key. *It's saying, "I'm wrong." Get out and go on to something else.*

In every stock, with every decision, day traders are competing against market makers. What advantages does a market maker have over an electronic trader?

Market makers know if they have 100,000 (shares) to buy or sell. We don't know that as day traders. We can see something moving and it looks like a great trade and all of a sudden, Goldman Sachs will be there on the offer and he won't move. He's got a half a million to sell. And then he'll start banging the bid and before you know it, you'd better get out or take a loss there.

It's a cat-and-mouse game, knowing when these market makers are for real and when they're not. Market makers will play tricks. Say Goldman has been a seller but he's sitting on the bid. And you're thinking maybe he's now a buyer. You take the offer and all of a sudden he starts hitting the bid. There is a stock, Manugistics, which went up $12 in one day on great earnings. You knew NationsBank Montgomery was the buyer. He would not allow the stock to go down. Every time Montgomery went to the bid, you'd go to the bid. If you didn't get hit on the bid, you'd take the offer and the stock would go up. If you can find who the player is in a particular stock, it makes things that much easier.

What clues appear on your screen that that suggest the market maker might be playing tricks?

Today, for instance, Deutsche Morgan Grenfell (DMGL) was the seller at Amazon on the offer. Then the stock pulled in, and DMGL goes to the bid. People think maybe he's turned here; I've got to buy it. So he got everybody to buy the stock and move up the price, and all of a sudden he went right back to the offer.

Did he have a buyer?

No. That's one of his tricks. There is a lot of new and scared money being traded out there. New guys will say, okay, he's no longer the seller, he's the buyer. So they buy right away, but he is still the seller. There's no evidence showing that he wasn't a seller.

So you held on. You didn't fall for the old bait and switch. What would you need to have seen to convince you that

the market maker indeed had turned a new leaf? After all, you're watching the action closely here—if he moves conclusively, you might jump to the opposite side yourself.

If I had seen that DMGL bought a thousand and another thousand, then it looks like he's starting to take a nibble or to cover a short. So I'll take a shot.

Market makers want day traders to perceive they're something they're not. For day traders, the stock market amounts to one big poker game. They want us to believe that they're a seller when they're really a buyer. The best trick is if they're really a buyer and they're on the offer. It means they have an order, they're buying stock on the bid from their customers, and as soon as the customers don't sell any more stock, they'll go high bid and run the stock up higher. In that case with DMGL where the guy is really a seller and he tries to run to the buy side and doesn't support the stock, you know he's still a seller until you see him actually buy stock.

But when Goldman Sachs has something, you don't go against him. Goldman usually shows his hand. If he's a seller, he's going to sell the stock. He's not going to play games in the market, because he has more clout and power. When Goldman Sachs does something, you usually want to be on the same side.

What exactly do you mean by "he"? Is that the company or the market maker?

The market maker in that particular stock. There are several hundred market makers out there.

What other bells and whistles tell you who the players are and how you might want to approach the market?

You see on the screen what market makers have been doing. Are there a lot of ECNs buying? Is there a lot of market maker buying and selling? Also you look for volume. You want to see a stock up nicely on good volume.

I'm primarily a bull trader. I feel the market is going to go up. But I am getting better at playing the short side as well. You really need to do both sides of the markets to be a short-term investor. You want to take advantage of the price swings. We always hope, being bull traders, that the market opens down. In the past when it opened down, it always rallied back. Our biggest problem is when the market opens up high—100 points—what do we do? So what I've been doing now is fading the opening—you try to get short on the opening and see how much stocks pull in. If they don't pull in a lot, you cover your short and get long because there is a good chance of a stock making higher highs. This is because market makers and pros sell the up opening, hoping to buy the stock back at the first sign of weakness. If there is no weakness, this is a sign that the buyers are still around and it naturally follows that the market makers will demand higher prices if they have to sell more. They may also be forced to cover the shorts that they established on the opening.

For instance, if Amazon.com opens up $3, I'll short it. If the market comes in and the stock isn't going down anymore, I'll put a bid in. You don't get hit, so you take the offer and get long.

So Amazon.com has been one of your core stocks. What are some other companies that appear regularly in your sights?

I'll also trade Microsoft and Dell, but I think they are too thick. There are dozens of market makers trading Dell,

Microsoft, and Intel. I traded Intel today and I thought I was going to go out of my mind. It took half an hour to make a quarter of a point on 2000 shares. My time is better spent trading Amazon and what I call thinner stocks.

It seems advantageous to trade stocks with fewer available shares—a thin "float," as it's called. You can be in and out of these stocks faster, and in this work, time really is money.

I think it's an advantage. Basically what I'm doing is just watching stock and watching for where the stock pulls in, where it goes up. You can figure out the trading range of that stock for that hour of the day. Every time it pulls in, you put a bid out, you get hit, then it goes back up. You sell it up ¼, ½ a point, and just go back and forth playing market maker.

The days of just buying with SOES or just taking the offer are gone. The majority of the people who are trading successfully are essentially acting as market makers. It reduces your risk and allows you to expand your time horizon. Say Amazon is $120¼ by ½. If I go and take 120½ stock, I paid a ¼ spread. And all of a sudden I see reds on my screen—meaning the stock is going down. Offers pile up and the bids start dropping and I'm like, "Oh God, if I don't hit the bid I'll lose a half a point." But if you buy the stock at $120¼ or $120 and five teenies and all of a sudden you see some reds, you say "I can hold a little longer." If it drops ⅛, ¼, it's no big deal since I haven't paid that spread.

Many day traders talk about buying on the bid rather than taking the offer. That's not something a typical retail investor can do. Essentially, you become like a market maker.

I'm being a market maker and taking the same risks they are. If I'm going to buy on the bid, I will have to buy into the weakness. In a stock with a quarter-point spread, I'm also not paying that initial $250. If I'm wrong on a 1000-share lot, I've paid that spread and if I don't hit the bid, I'll lose $500. But if you buy on the bid and it goes down ⅛—that's $125. So you can let a trade go against you a bit, while if you take the offer and pay the spread, you might not be willing to give a trade the time it needs to work in your favor.

Buying on the bid lets you save the spread instead of paying it. But there's always the chance that you won't get hit on the bid.

That's the thing. What happens every morning is if we want to get long, we don't want to pay the offer at the opening. The market makers will open a strong stock at a price where they are willing to make a sale or get short in anticipation that once the initial buy orders are filled, the stock is likely to pull back in. As it pulls in, just when you think the the sell-off is slowing down, you throw a bid in that's either on the bid or a teenie above. If you don't get hit and the market starts going back up, you say, "Okay, I'm not going to hit on the bid." So take the offer and pay the spread if you want to own the stock.

How do you distinguish the day trading you practice from people who use an online broker to buy a stock at 10 A.M. and sell it a point higher at 3 P.M.?

There's a big difference. They don't see what's going on throughout the day. They just see the price of the stock. They don't see who the players are, or that Merrill Lynch has a huge order. There are a lot of nuances in the market, whether it's the

S&P futures, the semiconductor index, the NASDAQ futures, the 30-year Treasury bond futures. There are so many variables to make the picture look right.

You mentioned giving a trade enough time to work for you. In this electronic day-trading world, what is your concept of time?

Time can be three minutes. You can make $1000 in 10 seconds if you catch the momentum right. For instance, the market fell the other day and I took some overnights home. I was down $19,000. The next day within 15 minutes I was up $23,000. I was playing 2000-, 3000-share lots. That's not the norm, but if you play it right, you buy Amazon on the bid, it kind of settles in there and then all of a sudden it makes its next move, which might be two or three minutes after you buy.

What is the value behind taking an overnight position in a stock? Why not simply end the day flat—with no longs or shorts and just your profit and loss statement as testimony to your trading skills?

If you have a stock that you lost money in and you're still long, do not go home with it. It's weak for a reason. *Never take home a loser.* You may consider going home long a stock that is moving in your favor a good amount, whether it's a half a point, three points—on greater than average volume. Or if it closes near its highest highs for the day on greater than average volume. That is a typical take-home on the long side. On the short side, when the stock is down, closes near its lowest lows on greater than average volume, there's a good chance that it's going to open up lower the next day.

Do you ride a winning position as long as you can?

You'd like to. *But you're never going to buy the bottom and sell the tops.* You have to say, "What do I want to make today?" Everybody's financial situation is different. When you're up money and you have a nice cushion, you can let trades ride longer or you can let losses go against you a little more. But when you are starting off or it's early in your career, you first have to build that cushion. That is so key.

It seems that the best way to build a cushion is just one trade at a time. That goes back to discipline and controlling your losses.

Keep yourself to a quarter-point loss. Don't keep getting long. When I started, I kept getting long in the semiconductors and they were in a bear market. I'd try to buy every dip, hoping to sell the rallies and there were none. What I should have been doing with every little rally is getting short, which I did the other day in Amazon. The market was strong, but every time it would turn up, Amazon wouldn't follow. I thought it was going to go down, so I shorted and it went from up $3 to down $3 that day.

So you want to go long in stocks that are participating in rallies. And when you find a stock that can't break out in a strong market, you short it. By watching how it trades, you can actually see the overhead resistance keeping the stock down.

You can. You do chart work. It's not foolproof, but it helps. I'm not a technician but I can read a chart, see where support is, where resistance is, where an all-time high is. I have always made a lot of money when a stock makes a new all-time high. You look at a chart and say, "Amazon's all-time high was $130." If it gets to $130, I'm going to buy because there's a good chance it will go up two or three more points, which in the right market it does. In a downmarket, what stocks will do is make a new high by an eighth of a point and sell off a point. You have to know when to press the pedal to the metal and when to put your foot on the brake.

At this point, you obviously know what to do in a trade and when to do it. That's important to success in any career. But why are you a better trader for your experiences? What personal qualities do you bring to work now that you didn't before?

It's discipline. I always thought I was the best trader. But my problem was discipline. *The key to being a good trader is admitting when you're wrong.* I am very stubborn. I would never admit I'm wrong on a trade. You've got to be able to change your opinion 30, 40 times during the day. You'll say, "I love the market," and get long. Then you'll feel, "I hate the market," two minutes later. So you'll get out of everything and get short. Flexibility is key to being a good short-term trader—that and not going for the home run constantly.

I'll also try to control my losses, manage my money better in terms of when to press the pedal, and not try to force things. And I play smaller. I used to buy 20 positions. Now I buy 2 or 3 positions in 2000- or 3000-share lots. Some people are long 10,000, flipping for quarters. That's not my game.

If you could give only one piece of advice based on the knowledge you've gained about day trading, what would it be?

Discipline is number one. Controlling your losses is key to not digging yourself into a hole. Do not be stubborn. If you get into something and your capital is limited in the beginning and it's not working, get out and get into something else. That was my biggest problem. I would get into a bunch of things and none of them would work. Meanwhile I'd miss three other stocks that were running. I wasn't being flexible enough. You have to be flexible. Change your opinion, and admit when you're wrong.

Tom Hendrickson
Know Yourself

"When people trade, they only see that which they want to see. I was a genius, and every piece of information that went against my position I just ignored. Of course, the most important information is the price."

A t 44, Tom Hendrickson is a battle-tested veteran of a business where longevity is scarce and you're considered only as good as your last winning streak. He started day trading in 1991 in a firm founded by Harvey Houtkin, one of the original SOES "bandits," leaving behind a traditional, predictable commercial law practice for the uncertainties of the stock market.

Hendrickson has never looked back. But he does turn inward. Besides day trading his own account, he is an armchair student of the psychology of trading—seeking to understand *why* he and his peers make the choices they do.

Are traders' motives purely financial? Hendrickson thinks not. Of course, day trading can produce a good living. But for some, self-worth is dependent on net worth. They define themselves by what they do, not who they are. Their trading and their identities become indistinguishable. And it only takes a few big-time trades for heads to swell fatter than wallets.

In fact, trading—the basic mechanics of buying and selling—is easy, Hendrickson contends. But when ego clouds the picture, trading becomes more difficult—and dangerous. Ego, he warns, is a day trader's worst enemy. Indifference and objectivity—the tempering, true keys to trading success—are acquired through discipline and over time.

Trading without ego is a tough order, Hendrickson concedes, but is ultimately liberating. One day, he admits, he hopes to reach that goal. For he says it's only when you understand yourself—what it is about trading that motivates and satiates you—that you finally can let go of emotional baggage and have a clear vision of why you trade and what you really want from it. To be sure, getting to this level is challenging; its rewards are not even immediately apparent. But then, for the first time, you see that day trading is a job, not an adventure.

■   ■   ■

Trial by fire seems to be standard in the course of a trader's development. How did your own initiation into trading play out?

I was tired of law. Many of my friends worked on Wall Street. One had traded futures for a large bank and was out on his own. He had the bank as a customer, acting as its broker and trading for himself. I had a little money, but not much, so I needed the leverage of futures. I set aside $15,000 to trade. Then someone I knew suggested that I look at the lumber chart. I saw that it went straight up and was starting to come down. He suggested I might want to short it. So I did. That's how I turned the account from $15,000 to $45,000.

It sounds like you just parachuted in and hit the target. That's a triumph, not a trial.

I continued to play lumber, only now at a bigger size. Instead of one or two contracts, it was five or ten contracts. Lumber only traded a couple of hundred contracts a day. The spreads were wide and the volume was thin. I was trying to hold on for longer moves—one or two weeks. Except if I thought lumber was going to $200 from $300, I wouldn't short it at $300 and wait for it to get to $200. If it got to $250 and started bouncing, I would cover my short and try to put it out again later. I got chopped up doing that. I was on the wrong side of the market and refused to admit that I was wrong. And I lost the entire $45,000.

It was too good to be true, after all. What was going through your mind to make you so stubborn?

I felt very insistent. Of course, I started doing more research and found fundamental reasons to justify my positions. Then I looked at the charts and found more reasons. I ignored the only real important piece of information—which was that the price was going against me. The market didn't care about my analysis one bit.

Even worse than the market not caring is believing that it does. The truth can be devastating.

It certainly can be. As well as expensive. Many traders get into this mind-set that causes them to hold onto losers. Those losers get out of hand, and they lose a lot of money.

You wind up without much to show for all the trading costs and the opportunity costs you endure.

And sanity costs.

Wait—there's no such thing as sanity cost.

There is in this business.

After losing their entire bankroll, as you did with the $45,000, most people would peel themselves off the floor and find something else to do. For you, there was always the law. But you decided to stick it out.

I didn't consider law an option. A friend was making a good living day trading and suggested I give it a try. Every day for three months I watched him and another guy and figured, this wasn't so hard. I could do this. So I borrowed some money from friends, borrowed from my credit cards as protection for their money, and started trading. I remember losing the first day, the second day, the third day. But I lost a little less each time. After that I started making money.

You're obviously a quick study if you can begin making money day trading after just three sessions.

At the time, day trading was a lot easier than it is now. Stocks would run a half point, the market makers would be short, and if you offered out the stock they were anxious to cover and would take you. I was able to support myself for about 18 months, and then they changed the SOES rules. You could trade only 500 shares instead of 1000, and you were no longer able to short on a downtick.

Just before the rule change, technology stocks were in a strong downtrend. I had what at the time was my best month ever—$60,000. I thought, this is great, I had finally figured it out and I'm on my way. So I continued to short everything. Of course, I ended up shorting the bottom of the market, and not having learned my lesson from commodities, I held on because

I was convinced these tech stocks were going lower. The bounce was irrational. I had the charts. I had the fundamentals.

But you no longer had the profits. You repeated the lumber trading mistake.

When people trade, they only see that which they want to see. I was a genius, and every piece of information that went against my position I just ignored. Of course, the most important information is the price. I mention this because I've just read *Zen in the Markets,* by Edward Toppel, which pounded into my head something I've known for a while but don't always realize: trading is very easy, but we make it very hard.

Traders are hard on themselves, you mean. They take a game with straightforward rules and complicate it.

We make it hard because we have an ego and want to be right. We analyze and form opinions and put our trade on. If it goes our way, we're geniuses. If it doesn't, we think there is something wrong with the market. We look for all sorts of reasons not to get out of a losing trade: the stock's almost at a major support point on the chart; I won't sell until it violates that support point—even though the trade has already gone further than our rules would dictate.

Ego then would be a trader's number one enemy?

Absolutely. The whole idea is to trade without ego. It's like in tennis. A shot comes; you run after it and hit a cross-court backhand, because that's what is appropriate to do. You do it without thinking. Your return clears the net by six inches and hits six inches within the baseline. Effective trading works much the same way.

What's the trading equivalent of hitting a sharp cross-court backhand?

It's doing it, knowing it, and not thinking about it. Even more so, it's not being tied to the outcome. If you focus on what direction you think the market should go and how much money you should make on a trade, it doesn't work. You're not able to listen to what the market is telling you.

So the essence here is to focus on the stocks and not on yourself. If you're absorbed in ego and self-gratification, probably you're trading for the wrong reasons. Trading then defines your identity, instead of simply being a part of it.

Exactly. There are self-esteem goals. If I make winning trades, I am a good and worthy person. People will love me. If I lose, I am no good. Nobody will love me. That, I think, goes on a lot. Not that most traders ever think about it so deeply.

Obviously, you've given a fair amount of thought to the psychology of trading.

I find it fascinating. Psychologists have done research on how people react to probabilities. People were given a hypothetical bet and told, "These are your odds of winning or losing." If they had an opportunity to increase their winnings at the risk of losing what they had already won, most people didn't want to take the bet, even if the odds were in their favor. They would rather take the money in their pocket than roll the dice. But, when the experiment was reversed—when people were told they had a loss and there's a slight chance of getting it back, except the odds are they will lose more—most wanted to roll the dice. Unfortunately, this is not consistent with successful trading.

You're referring to a famous study that illustrates a mental condition called "loss aversion." Put simply, people hate losing more than they enjoy winning. That's why the first bet is unattractive, while the second bet offers an appealing chance to erase a loss. But how do these psychological tests relate to day trading?

It says that we are hardwired to cut our winners short and to gamble with our losers, which violates the two main rules of day trading: let winners run and cut losses short. It's our natural instinct to do things incorrectly in trading. If something goes against us, we hold onto it in the hope it comes back. That's the wrong thing to do. It makes it very difficult for the average trader to make money. First of all, the average trader isn't even aware that his instincts, which serve him well in so many other areas, are wrong for trading. And even when you do know, it's still hard to go against those instincts.

Many traders, in fact, refer to their work as a mental exercise, or they speak of getting "psyched" for the trading day. Without actually examining it, they really are addressing their own psychology.

We are taught growing up and in school to use our minds to manipulate our environment to get what we want. In my own training as a lawyer, there was a certain result I wanted, and I had to do whatever I could within the bounds of the law to get that result. To support my position, I would do research; I would do discovery of the other side to try to elicit facts, and I would argue persuasively to judges and juries.

This cause and effect—if X happens, then Y should happen—doesn't work in trading. In fact, it goes to your detriment. If it's cloudy and the wind starts to kick up, it's probably going to rain. But if news comes out on a stock that you think is bullish for the stock, it's not necessarily so.

So unlike in a courtroom, you're not able to argue your case before the market.

You can argue as much as you want, and when the market has all of your money, it will tell you to go home.

It must be unsettling to have a legal background and be in a situation where both judge and jury—the market—are deaf to your well-reasoned pleas.

It's very difficult, because I enjoy doing analysis and being right. That makes me money sometimes, but there are far more important skills to being a successful trader: let winners run; cut your losses; always follow your rules. You can add money management to that list—which means to bet only a set amount on any one idea. It's a great rule. But most of the people I've seen in the business don't have enough capital to bet only 5 percent of their money on one idea. So they are always betting 100 percent. Actually we're leveraged two-to-one, so we're betting as much as 200 percent long or short. Leverage is great when it's going your way. But you don't realize how fast your money disappears when it's going against you.

It's striking that such a fiercely independent effort like day trading should have even one hard-and-fast rule. Solo operators like you must often see these rules as meant to be broken.

In fact, sometimes you make money if you don't follow the rules. But it sets a bad example. A trader who has made money this way tends to break the rules more often. He may make $10 when this works, but he's going to lose $100 each time it doesn't. Yet all he will remember is the $10 he made. It's hard to extinguish this type of behavior once it's learned.

With regard to learned behavior, you contend that day trading is easy, and the real secret to success is controlling ego. What's so basic about trading?

It's relatively easy to look at a chart and identify a stock in an uptrend or a downtrend. If the stock is in an uptrend, buy it on the bid with a specific, reasonable stop-loss in place and let it ride until the trend changes. We don't do that. I owned Dell a year and a half ago in the $20s (it later went to $120). I made a half a point on the trade.

Sounds like a layup. What's the big deal? Day traders aren't supposed to care about a stock's price, valuation, or direction. You can always jump back and forth.

That's true. But not being capitalized enough at the time, and not yet being the trader I could be, I saw that half-point profit in Dell and thought I should take my money off the table. Yes, I could always buy it back. But by getting out of the trade, a gap opened. I would have made a lot more money buying Dell and just holding on, following the trend.

Why is following the trend so important?

You have to swim with the tide. The stock is not going up because you buy 1000 shares of it. It's only going up if many people with many dollars are buying the stock. You want to be on the same side as those dollars. That's what we try to do in short-term trading—identify a stock where money is going in today, buy on any dip, and wait for the big buyers to push the price up.

What goals have you established for yourself to climb to a higher level of expertise?

My current goal is to try to trade with less of an ego and not be attached to the results. When I'm on, I can make a ton of money. When I'm off, I can lose a ton. I've been off lately and now I'm just trying to listen to what the market is telling me it's doing, rather than what I think it should do.

What kind of commitment will it take from you to achieve these goals?

It involves making a conscious effort to dispassionately look at what I'm doing; to say, "This looks like a strong stock today, I like the chart, I'll buy it." If it goes against me, I'll get out quickly. If it goes in my favor, I'll buy more as long as general market conditions look like they'll continue up.

A new day trader asks for your advice on how to succeed in this business. What's your answer?

Read books dealing with the psychology of trading. It is very much a mental game. It's not against the market; it's not against other traders. It's a game against yourself. Understanding that might at least give people an idea of what they are really up against. It's a very difficult business.

Yet market makers and rival traders would enjoy nothing more than to lighten your wallet. Certainly you're competing against them.

Having the discipline to cut your losers and let your winners run is a game you play with yourself. Ego, fear, and greed
will all conspire against you. If you're having a crummy month
and you get into a trade, and all of a sudden you've made half
a point on it, you'll be more tempted to try to close out that
trade and bank that half point. But if that stock is strong and
the market is strong, the right thing to do is to let that winner
run. What typically happens is that you take the half-point
profit and then watch the stock go up another half point. You
say, "I'm not going to buy it at $34 a share; I just sold at $33½,"
and by the end of the day the stock is at $39. Then you kick
yourself for not holding onto it.

**But why kick yourself if you make $500 for a few minutes
of work, especially when you can set up the same quick
hit time and again? Do you regret missed opportunities in
the market?**

It depends on how hard I'm being on myself. Some days I
can be easy and say I just wasn't following the rules and if I
did, I could have held onto that trade longer. And the next time
I will follow the rules. Other times I'm very hard on myself:
"You stupid idiot. What's the matter with you?" That's generally not very helpful.

**You conceded that the market isn't being so good to you
just now—you've been "off," as you put it. Are you dwelling
on this slump or concentrating on ways to get back in the
groove?**

My primary focus is to get out of it by being small and listening to what the market tells me to do. When I really listen,

I can hear it and it's clear. I'm not thinking about money at all. Thinking about money can be deadly. I just want to make a couple of good trades a day. And when I really focus, I can do that. I can come in and make money, and that's what I've been starting to do lately.

How are you able to listen to what the market tells you? What noise does that animal make?

It's hard to put into words. You watch price actions. You see how strong stocks really are. If the Dow is up 100 points and the NASDAQ is up 25 points, then Intel, Dell, and Cisco had better be up a point or two. If they're not, the market is telling you that it's not as strong as the averages would suggest. The troops are marching but the generals aren't. The troops will eventually go where the generals are. If the generals are retreating, the troops will soon follow.

Are the clues always so clear?

No, they rarely are. I don't know any way to describe it other than to watch price action. When the averages make new highs or the stocks you're watching are up on the day, are they making new highs also? If they all are, then the market is very strong. You just buy everything and hold on. If the averages are making new highs and major stocks are not rallying at all with them, then the market is certainly weaker than it looks. Go in. Make your bet. Cut your losses short and let your winners run. Again, it's easy—until we complicate it.

Many traders set a target of making a certain amount of money each day—$500, $1000. Do you have a specific dollar figure in mind when you trade?

No, I find that counterproductive. That's like trying to hit a cross-court backhand and have the ball land six inches from the baseline. When I do that, I hit into the net. If I just hit when it comes to me, my shots are much better. If your goal is to make $1000 a day and you're almost there—the stock only has to go up another ⅛ of a point to get that $1000—you might hold that position even though the S&P futures have just dropped and NASDAQ futures are following. Inevitably, the bid on the stock will start to drop as well. From making nearly $1000, you end up making $200 on the day—if you're lucky.

So right now you're satisfied just to get a couple of good trades in each day.

I'm happy now to focus on good entry points. Say I'm bidding for a stock on a pullback, somebody hits me, and the price doesn't drop much below where I bought. That's a good intraday support point. Hopefully the stock will rally from there. That trade tells me I'm on, I'm focusing, I'm seeing things correctly.

At the worst point in your trading experience, when things looked darkest, how much money were you down?

The actual number is not important. I've been basically flat broke and wondering where the next month's rent is going to come from. It's very hard to trade from that position. There is an old axiom that "scared money never wins." In addition to telling new traders to read all those books, I would tell them to have a lot of money in the bank. With scared money, your ego gets involved too much. If the loss doesn't matter to you, then it's easier to take. It's when you can't afford to lose the money that it's harder to take the loss, because you really need that stock to come back at least to your entry point so you can get out even.

Since you've experienced downturns in your luck before, you must have a sense of how to regain your footing.

I've had them and I've been able to come back. I have no doubt that I will again by sticking to the rules and not focusing on results. Of course, that's hard to do because trading is all about results. I don't know how to surmount that. I know what the rules are. I know what I should do. It's very hard to do that all the time. One can always find reasons why you don't have to follow the rules.

Ultimately, the rules catch up with you.

They do. That's why many people come into this business and a good percentage leave. Very few are able to make a living. And even fewer make the big money.

James Crane-Baker
Admit Mistakes

---

*"In gambling, when you let go of the dice you
don't have control. Good traders are not gamblers,
good traders stay in control."*

Many investors and traders pore over company reports,
price charts, and other promising market tools, spong-
ing up information on a stock until it seems that every last
detail is locked inside their heads.

For James Crane-Baker, stock trading comes from the
gut. Today's share volume and price are the only history he
cares about. Who's on the bid right now? Who's at the offer?
Do buyers or sellers have the upper hand? Crane-Baker sizes
up the situation in an instant, then decides to go long or short.
If he's slow to act, a rival electronic day trader—maybe even
the trader next to him in his lower Manhattan office—is going
to take those shares first. Crane-Baker knows that to win his
specialized game, he's got to stay one step ahead of a fast,
expert crowd.

Crane-Baker, 26, didn't know much about trading when
he started, other than it seemed like something he thought

he'd be good at. That come-what-may confidence is typical of many successful day traders, and a valuable asset once they've mastered the rudiments of timing and navigating a trade. Crane-Baker also is known for being fiercely independent, a quality he shares with many of his fellow day traders, and he's unafraid to have his own opinion—that gut feeling—to guide him through a position.

At times Crane-Baker will misjudge a call, of course, and wind up flat on the wrong side of a stock. That's when traders are really put to the test. Admitting the mistake is key—many traders have enough trouble with that—but can they recognize the error quickly enough to keep the loss small?

Crane-Baker knows how important this skill is to keeping profits and preserving capital. If a trade is going against him, he's dashing for the exit even before the alarm sounds. If he isn't quick enough, the market will sock him hard. But once he's safely out of a losing position, he looks back and tries to understand what got him into trouble. Were circumstances out of his control, or could he have made better choices? And that's another edge Crane-Baker has over many traders: not only does he readily admit mistakes, he learns from them, too.

■　■　■

You already have a couple of years' worth of day-trading experience under your belt. Obviously, the chase hasn't bored you yet. What surprising lesson have you learned about the business that has most influenced your trading style?

I thought day trading would be more mathematical. In fact, stock trading is all crowd psychology. As a trader, you're

trying to predict the future by watching the crowd and trying
to stay one step ahead. And if you're like me, you're literally
trying to anticipate the next minute's move. You don't care
about the fundamentals. I'm not a fundamental trader. I'm not
a technician. I know a bit about technical analysis just from
being in the business, but it's not part of my game. I use it for
basics, like when a stock makes a new 52-week high or breaks
into an uptrend. You can call me a discretionary trader. I have
no technical formula for getting into my trades. It's up to my
own discretion. Basically, it's gut trading. I'm just watching the
tape. What I mean is that I'm watching trading volume and the
prints. Every stock trade prints to the tape. I'm also watching
market makers, electronic communications networks (ECNs)
like Instinet, and other day traders.

**All of this action happens extremely fast. You can't be
caught flat-footed.**

You have to be ahead of the stampede and also anticipate
where it's going next. For example, you watch Dell Computer
run up several dollars, and you anticipate that the crowd is
excessively long and there really aren't many more buyers. So
you sell the stock short. Then the crowd begins to sell at the
offer and the stock—like a roller coaster—goes back downhill.
Sometimes it can get scary. If you're wrong, the crowd is not
going to be with you. These moves can happen violently or
slowly—it depends on the stock. Institutions, market makers,
ECNs, day traders—everybody's moving the stock around. The
players and their order change quickly—within 5 or 10 minutes. Sometimes you can watch the battle between market
makers. Today, for instance, a market maker for Merrill Lynch
was selling a lot of Dell stock, while a market maker from

Goldman Sachs was pushing it up. You could watch the two battle. Merrill won out.

You could watch the battle, or you could take sides. What did you do?

I preferenced Merrill for a 5000-share block and he filled me in a second, no problem. When a stock is going up and a market maker is trying to hold it down, he is the last one on the offer before the stock lifts. I had the opinion that Dell was going up, but Merrill is a force to be reckoned with. Still, I decided to trade against him. Even though I saw Merrill as a big seller, I thought that there was enough upward pressure from the Standard & Poor's 500 stock index futures that the shorts in Dell would cover and push him up a bit. Liquidity to the downside was also good. There were a lot of bidders for the stock. The risk was definitely worth the potential reward. I thought 5000 shares was an adequate risk, not too excessive.

In the short run I won—I sold it up ⅜ of a dollar. That was a nice clip on 5000 shares. But eventually it went back down. Merrill was right. He was just dealing with a lot of share volume, so he sold at every level all the way up.

Did the stock run more after you sold?

A little. But you have to get out where you can, not when you'd like.

Is Dell Computer one of the core stocks you trade?

Whatever is hot and in play is essentially my core. When we had a great run-up in the Internet stocks, that's where I was trading. I'll also trade the market stocks, just because they move.

What are the market stocks?

Dell, Microsoft, Cisco Systems, Intel—big tech companies that make up a large portion of the NASDAQ market capitalization. They are the market. The stocks of these big companies have a lot of players in them and the highest daily trading volume. So if you open up the newspaper and look at the most active list, you normally see Cisco and Dell. But I also like stocks that are highly volatile and just happen to be the most active on a given day. I'd like to have been in those. By watching the market and the headlines that prompt stocks to move—you can find them.

You say that "gut trading" is your game. You watch action and news, and since you're experienced enough to see beyond the obvious, seemingly innocent tidbits hit you head-on. But many rival traders have similar, or even better, skills. So when you see the iron is hot—knowing they do, too—what's your move?

Buy stock. But it's tricky to determine if the news is actually going to make the stock go higher or just be a fake-out. Then you have to judge how much stock you really want, and whether you want to pay through the offer to get it. My edge is that I can make a decision quickly and be right. I don't bother with the bigger picture so much. And when the market is really hauling, I can take big clips out of it. Things move really fast, but I'm disciplined. I don't like to have big down drops in my equity, and I combine that with fast decision making.

Traders and investors alike struggle mightily to build discipline and finely tuned instinct; many never reach this

level. You apparently have. How did you settle on your particular brand of "gut-level" day trading?

I stumbled into this line, and it really suits me. While I'm making fast decisions, I have my own opinion. I'm also comfortable changing that opinion and learning from my mistakes. You're going to be wrong, and it's going to happen every day. That's something you have to deal with. If you can't learn from your mistakes and admit you're wrong, day trading probably isn't right for you. Failure confronts you constantly; you just have to keep going.

True, everyone has scrapes and falls. Just because someone possesses strong discipline and keen instinct doesn't mean they'll never get hurt.

It's been a learning process since I started trading in April 1996. I'm still learning about myself and how to deal with the market, and probably always will be. Some days you're really calling the market. You buy the bottom, the stock rips up, you sell the top. You're getting filled at great prices because you're anticipating moves and are ahead of other people. Other days you're slow. You buy the top and sell at the bottom. Those days you have to trade in smaller volume and try to understand what's going on in the market, because you're not seeing something correctly. You have to learn from those days in order to keep them to a minimum.

Presence of mind probably gives you greater confidence to pick yourself up at once and scramble back on board.

It helps that I try not to swing for the fences every day. When you're always swinging for the fences, you're going to fall down. Just hit singles on a daily basis. When you are batting well, then swing for the fences—but you really have to know yourself and understand when to pull back and when to let go.

How are you a better trader now than when you started?

Other than not knowing anything when I started? I learned a lot about discipline and risk, to take profits when I have them, to keep those profits, and to correctly read when to trade and when to sit on the sidelines. You're going to end up on the losing side of some trades, and you have to learn to understand what you did wrong and try not to let it happen again.

When I started, for instance, I traded wide-spread stocks, and these are very risky. Some spreads were like $2 wide. It's too much risk, especially for a new trader. Other times I would have $1 profit on 1000 shares in a stock and not take it, and end up losing money on the trade. The traders who were helping me out would say, "You had the money—you should have taken it." Even if I had a quarter in the stock, they were telling me, "That's $250—book that profit."

It's probably fair to suppose that you lost more than $1000 in the beginning.

I lost $50,000 of a $100,000 base. I started in April and stopped losing money in the middle of July. It took me until then to say I think I understand what's going on here. I can do this. Until then I was just trying to figure it out.

What you call a "learning process," others would describe as torture. Going to work day after disappointing day must have been excruciating.

It definitely tries your patience and your ego. Fear and greed are constantly battling each other. You're scared to lose money but you want to make money. You have to balance those two, because you don't want one to control the other. If you let fear overcome greed, you're never going to make money. If greed overcomes you, it's never enough, and you're probably going to lose all of your money.

Things gradually went from "I think I can" to "I know I can." I never really doubted myself. I heard the rules and eventually started to apply them. Since then, I've only lost money in one month. That was when they switched the SOES rules, so we had to get used to that, and I had a bad trade in a stock that halted on me. I was short and all of a sudden it halted and was taken over like $20 higher. I lost about $15,000.

You got hit for $15,000 on a single trade, and yet you're speaking so calmly about it. Which stock was the culprit?

I can't really remember.

That's extraordinary. A trade socks you for $15,000 and you can't recall which stock you were playing. Apparently, you don't lose sleep over setbacks.

No. This had nothing to do with my trading ability. I was trading the stock great. The shares were very volatile that day and I was trading the volatility. Obviously, something was going to happen. I was in the right. I was actually $3 in the money and then the stock halted. That's going to happen sometimes. But I would do the same thing today. I can't worry about stocks halting.

The trades I remember are ones where I've made a poor decision. My worst day ever, I proceeded to make bigger bets that the market was going up. It never did. I was long 25,000 Intel, and at one point I was down about $50,000. I lost about $30,000 that day—probably $20,000 of that on Intel alone.

You're $50,000 in the hole, and the closing bell is nowhere near to being rung. This isn't play money you've lost. For many people, it's like blowing an entire year's salary in one morning. At that point, what thoughts and emotions are running through your head?

I'm not losing my cool. I'm not panicking. I was wrong. Now what's the best way to deal with the situation? I thought we were going to rally big and we just stayed flat. If I'd been right, I could have made $250,000. So I had to control the situation. I got out of the positions as best I could, and then tried to make a little of it back.

Those experiences stay in my mind more than the freak instances of stocks halting. It's probably happened 10 or more times that a stock has halted like that and I've gotten smacked in it. It burns you up, but it's out of your control and has nothing to do with your trading ability.

You were long many thousands of shares and trapped on the wrong side of the trade. Not a pretty spot to be in, to be sure, but why did you close out your positions rather than take them home overnight in the hope that the next day would be better?

It's not my style. I don't feel comfortable. When the market is closed, the market is closed. I like to be flat. Not that I haven't gone home with positions overnight, but it's not where I make most of my money. I feel like I lose control when the market is closed. It's not a skill I've developed.

Developing and improving ability is what all novice day traders strive for, though few succeed. Once these skills are acquired, do traders then reach a plateau, or do you find that trading is in fact a continuous evolution?

I'm evolving now, as always. You have to adjust your style, because the market is always changing. You have to change with it and improve. I'm more comfortable trading larger-sized positions than when I started. Right now I'm working on being able to ride market trends a bit longer. Sometimes when you're trading larger blocks—5000 or 10,000 shares—you need a bigger move in order to get in and out. The liquidity you need isn't always there. Market makers won't trade with you first. They're filling their customers, not providing liquidity to you. We're the last resort. So you have to hold through the jiggle in the stock a little bit more.

There are so many day-trading rules and insights, it can be difficult to keep track. Each signpost has meaning, some more than others. The best traders understand the basics plus a few extras—you and others have highlighted these points in detail. But one trader's priority is not necessarily another's; it seems almost that each trader follows the rules according to, well, their own rules.

New people ask, "How do you make money?" They want to know the rules. They want me to lay it down for them on paper how I make money. But it's impossible for me even to write a list of hard, fast rules without saying that I haven't broken every single one of them—probably that day, even. You have to know when the rules apply and when they don't, and that's difficult. That can't be taught. You just have to feel your way.

Still, you must have a top rule, a guiding precept to live by. What is it?

Discipline—not getting out of control in trading. You have to control your losses, keep your head, not try to swing for the fences with huge bets. You discipline yourself by saying, "I'm here to hit singles every day." You know when it's appropriate to take on larger risks. Some people lose their discipline and overtrade. They take more risk than they can handle. Sometimes you can just go nuts and trade away and lose yourself. So you really have to be able to control your emotions. And learn to play market maker—buying stocks on the bid and selling them on the offer instead of buying offers and hitting bids. Then you pocket the spread. It's another way to reduce your risk.

Some observers might dismiss day trading as merely a bull-market phenomenon—at what other time do people forgo traditional careers and opportunities for the alluring, fast money of the markets? Once this bull dies, they contend, expect day trading's popularity to go with it. Would you agree?

People who say day traders aren't going to make money in downmarkets are naive. They don't understand what we're doing. Day traders on the NASDAQ most closely resemble pit traders in Chicago—except we use a computer. I make money whether the market is up or down. That's fine; I go to cash every night. A flat market is what scares me—low volatility in the S&P futures and stocks. But I don't think that's going to happen. There is too much money in the market and on the sidelines for the market to just trade sideways.

The perception that market volatility is here to stay seems rather self-fulfilling from your perspective, for certainly it's been noted that the surge in day-trading activity has exacerbated the market's often-dramatic swoons.

That's a lot of market-maker propaganda. They had something good, so they try to paint us as the enemy. Essentially, they're trying to box us out. They want to be the big players, but we're the ones trading every day and trying to make a living from the market volatility. Still, they want to exclude us and protect their spread.

You launched into day trading virtually right out of college. It seems you knew what you wanted, and now apparently you've got it. But if you weren't trading, would any other career hold a similar attraction?

I don't know. I definitely wouldn't do anything on Wall Street other than trading. Other aspects of trading interest me, like trading the commodities pits or seeing what it's like as a market maker. But I really enjoy the independence of this job, and since I've been doing it for a couple of years, working for somebody else would be tough. I like the fact that it's like my own business. Most people go to work and have a list of things they have to get done. They do them and then get a paycheck every week. That wouldn't interest me. I like a challenge. Day trading definitely challenges me; I see new things every day. It's rewarding, and it's not like any other job that I can imagine.

To say that day trading is rewarding is an understatement. Highly successful traders make more money than some corporate chief executives—and you only work between 9:30 A.M. and 4 P.M.

Day trading is not so much about the money; it's more about playing the game. That's what draws people to it. Playing the game, being competitive, and wanting to be correct in the market. It feels good to be one step ahead of the crowd. Day trading is basically a big game for adults. The money is just a way to keep score. I dislike it when people equate the stock market with gambling. I'm not a gambler myself. I know some people in the market are. I don't think that gambling and trading go hand in hand. *In gambling, when you let go of the dice, you don't have control. In trading, you always have control. Good traders are not gamblers; good traders stay in control.*

Are you satisfied with the way you're trading now, or are there new ways of approaching the market that you would like to master?

I don't think I'm ever satisfied. I always want to do better. There is always some way to have made a little bit more. In some regard, you should be appreciative of what you've made. In other regards, I'm always trying to improve my trading and change it according to what the market is showing me.

Jim Shaw
Develop Seasoned Judgment

"Day trading is the church of what's happening now."

The single greatest day-trading epiphany might have been when Jim Shaw, $83,000 in the hole after five torturous months of unrelenting losses, plaintively turned his palms to the heavens and had what he calls "a coming to Jesus." Shaw felt he was being tested through a trial by fire. Here he was, a competitive sort who always tried hard and rarely failed, flat on his back with just a prayer.

Shaw, 35, trades from an office in Atlanta with several traders and partner Brad Frericks, an association first forged in high school in rural Quincy, Illinois. Shaw studied accounting in college and worked briefly for consulting giant Arthur Andersen. All the while he longed to become a securities trader, but the closest he got after receiving an M.B.A. was a position analyzing mortgage-backed bonds for brokerage firm Duff & Phelps.

Day trading, with its democratizing influences, gave Shaw entry to a formerly exclusive club. He embraced day trading full-time in May 1996, working out of his house on a remote electronic system which provided the same Level 2 quotes that NASDAQ market makers see. They were two inexperienced traders, Shaw and Frericks, and they suffered mightily for it. At one point, Shaw recalls, he and Frericks would compete to see who lost the least amount of money in a day.

Maybe it was divine intervention, perhaps it was plain soul-searching, but Shaw ultimately found salvation. He began to make smaller trades and think about booking smaller gains. Besides a window on Level 2 quotes, he found a deep level of humility in trading that he had never known. And as a result, he claims, he started to make money.

On those frustrating days when nothing is going right, Shaw remembers that lean time and its lessons, and reminds himself to be humble. It's a way for him to focus, to regain authority. An instinctive trader by nature, it took repeated beatings before he learned that shooting from the hip is no way to hit a bull's-eye. Instinct is a crucial piece of the trader's game, to be sure. But great traders, Shaw is convinced, also add discipline and seasoned judgment to their finely tuned reflexes.

Seasoned judgment? You're not born with it. It evolves over time and through experience. And it's difficult to have confidence about your judgment without first mastering discipline and instinct. Together, these qualities make a three-point play, and a trader with seasoned judgment is likely at the top of his game. How do you recognize it? Think of it this way: once you develop seasoned judgment, even a losing trade becomes profitable.

■   ■   ■

As you describe it, your first months of day trading were purgatory, if not worse. Now that you're safely beyond that point, can you recall some of the mistakes you made?

I started in May of 1996 with about $200,000 in my trading account and another $100,000 invested in stocks. During the next five months, I ended up losing about $83,000 in the trading account. Of the other $100,000, I probably lost $50,000. Those investment losses weighed heavily on me when I was trading. I advise any trader to put your other investments in mutual funds. Don't be worrying about your personal portfolio at the same time you're trying to trade. It really affects your day trading. You lose objectivity. *Day trading is the church of what's happening now.* With day trading, I want to be there with the market. If the market is selling off, I probably want to be short. If it's going up, I want to be in strong stocks that are going up.

Keeping one eye on a trade and the other on portfolio stocks is a real distraction. You take time and focus away from trading to check on the long-term investments, and both suffer. Curiously, many mutual fund managers also feel conflicted about their job and their own account.

You just hurt more and more. Do I sell it? Do I hold it? It clouds your judgment. For example, this week I lost probably $50,000 in an investment. I was hoping the market was going to come back, but things sold off instead.

Was that $50,000 loss from one of your trades?

No, it's an investment. Every time this happens—I've probably done it three times now—I say I'll never do that again. Then I get back in that trap. You just don't want to have other things going on that can rock your world as a trader.

So it's hard to trade and invest simultaneously.
Unless you're in mutual funds.

Early on, you reached a turning point where some difficult but meaningful lessons were learned. It started when you were down $83,000 of your $200,000. That's a pretty depressing place to be.
I lost money in May 1996 when I started. June was actually an up month by a fluke. In July I got hammered; August I got hammered. In September I lost more money, and again in October. Toward the end of October I was down about $30,000 for just that month, which was the world to me then. All of a sudden, I'm down like $83,000. I almost cried. I had a coming to Jesus. It was one of those, "Look, I've never really failed at anything that I've really tried my hardest at, and I've tried my hardest and I just can't get it." I got my resume ready, but I also got humble and said I'm just going to try to make $1000 a day. That's all I want to do.

What were you trying to do with trades before this compromise—smack the long ball every time?
I was always trying to swing a big bat, and it always got me in trouble. There are three things that make a good trader: discipline, instinct, and seasoned judgment—which is an offshoot of discipline and instinct.

Which of those three crucial qualities did you bring to the plate when you started—discipline, instinct, or seasoned judgment?

I initially had good instincts. But I also had bad instincts that defeated me. New traders often won't go for it. They'll sit and watch stocks that are moving, and they won't lose much money, but they're never really going to make a lot of money either. From the get-go I would always trade stocks that were moving. But I was trading against good market makers. They were eating my lunch.

So you didn't understand two of the most important trading rules—when to fold 'em and when to take the money.

Discipline was my problem. I didn't let myself walk away with the profits. I would be up $7000, which was a big day for me, and end the day down $4000. George West was watching me trade one day. And I said, "I blew it. I had a good morning and I threw the money away." He said, "Yeah, I sat behind you and watched." He wasn't impressed. There's a million guys who can make money. But not many walk away with it.

And keeping profits is what counts.

The biggest turning point was when I really got humble and said I'm not trying to make a lot of money, I'm just trying to make a little and walk out of here.

A thousand dollars a day is not exactly a vow of poverty. But it was a touchstone nonetheless.

I don't know how I had the courage to press the keys, but the next three days I made $15,000, and all of a sudden I was only down by about $68,000 at the end of October. That was a huge win. I fought my way through November and made $15,000 for the month—my first winning month since June. In December I was trading at home and in one day made $25,000. I got a little bit lucky, everything clicked, and it was "Wow!" So by the end of the year I was down $33,000, which was an incredible win.

Now that you're more successful, whatever happened to the $1000 a day reminder?

Whenever I have a down day or two down days in a row, I go back to being conservative. Maybe it's more like $3000 a day now, but that's what I go back to when I get humble. It's the philosophy that works more than the absolute dollar amount—"Come in, make a little money, you don't have to kill 'em." When you have that attitude, you're humble, you're cautious, you're not trying to beat the market. When a trader says, "I'm going to make $20,000 today and get it all back," 9 times out of 10 he's going to have a big losing day because he is too aggressive, too cocky, too sure of himself. *The market has a way of punishing arrogance.*

Some people might regard humility in day trading as being weak. You see it as a strength.

Every day I go in, I'm a little nervous, I'm a little bit afraid. I trade better like that than I did when I was more cocksure. But when I get there, I go for it. I'm not just sitting. Trading is like athletics. Before a game, everybody is a little queasy. Emotions are running high. That's how I get before every day of trading.

Some apprehension before the trading day begins actually forces you to center yourself, to overcome your fears

and doubts. Once you are centered, the day or the game goes according to how well you play and nothing more. After all, you're a professional. You know what's needed to win.

Exactly. You get in your rhythm by kind of centering yourself beforehand and letting the game play itself out. That's what it is. I definitely do things to get myself in that mode.

How do you gear yourself for the trading day? You may be nervous about what can go wrong, but that doesn't keep you from coming to work. You just do your best. But centering yourself is more than just taking a deep breath, walking through the door, and shouting, "It's showtime!"

I watch CNBC in the morning. Then I feel I haven't missed anything. I feel grounded knowing what state the markets are in. If I haven't caught up on what's out there, I feel like I'm trading naked. If there's a major trend, I don't want to do the wrong things because I didn't know information that I should have. Then I drive to work thinking about my strategy for the day.

As you review strategy and a game plan, are there any mental exercises you undertake?

I'm thinking about what I want to accomplish. If I want to have a big day, I try to talk myself into it. I say, "Let's go in and make a little bit of money." I will try to do that on a continual basis, especially after down days. Like this week—Monday I made a couple of thousand, Tuesday I lost $12,000. Wednesday I came in expecting to be small, just trying to make a little bit of money. I was taking profits all day, getting out when I could, not when I had to. And I caught the turn in the market and ended up making $35,000. The next two days after were also good. Thursday I made $20,000 and Friday I made about $16,000.

Which stocks have you been trading to make that kind of money?

Amazon.com is my favorite stock. At the end of the month when I pull up my P&L (profit and loss) on individual stocks, a lot of my money comes from Amazon.

How many stocks do you follow?

Probably 200.

So you have a working knowledge of 200 stocks. What do you know about them? Fundamentals? Trading patterns?

Trading patterns. I definitely chart, but not all 200. When I say 200, it's not that I notice them all the time. I'll be playing the action but I follow them on a weekly basis. If I see them moving in one direction, I'll pull up a chart and see if I like it. If I do, sometimes I'll buy it and hold it for a couple of days.

Of that 200, there is probably a select group that you've really studied hard. How many stocks make up that core?

About 40.

These are stocks that most likely you've followed for a long time. You know them well and are comfortable trading them.

I didn't say "I know." I only have an opinion. Never say you know, because whenever you say that you get whacked.

That's fair. Let's say then that you have an educated sense of these companies and their trading patterns. Before the

opening bell, do you choose the stocks you're going to play, or do you get a feel as the day evolves?

In the morning, I'm looking for what I think is going to move for the day, and I'm going to try to be long. From listening to the market, from seeing where things are bid on the opening, I'll have an opinion as to what may be moving. I try to play the action because the action is where the most money is. When I say action, I mean that if Internet stocks are moving in $12 ranges, I'll probably play those versus a chip stock with a $2 range.

By $12 ranges, do you mean the gap between the high price and low price for the day?

Exactly. If there is a $12 range, which has been pretty common in Internet stocks, I want to be playing those. Somewhere in that $12 I've got to be able to take a buck here and a buck there.

When you listen to the market, as you put it, what are you hearing?

I'm constantly looking at the relative strength of NAS-DAQ Composite Index compared to the Dow, the NASDAQ 100, and the direction of the S&P 500 futures. If I see the Dow up 40 and the NASDAQ Composite up 20, for instance, I know that the real strength of the market is in NASDAQ stocks. The NASDAQ is up more in percentage terms than the Dow.

If the Dow Jones Industrial Average is up more in points than the NASDAQ index, wouldn't that signal a stronger Dow? Or is there an easy ratio that we should know about?

You are looking for the percentage move. If the Dow is five times the level of the NASDAQ Composite, you take the NASDAQ index and simply multiply by five. So the NASDAQ up 20 should equate to a Dow up 100. Here, the Dow is up only 40, so the NASDAQ is stronger than the Dow. When the S&P futures get strong, I'm going to look for NASDAQ stocks that I think are going higher. If we have a stronger Dow than NAS-DAQ, my strategy will probably be to short NASDAQ rallies, and also be very stock-specific.

Strengthening S&P futures indicate that money is coming into the market—specifically the Standard & Poor's 500 stock index. It's a way to see where the cash is flowing. And, of course, you want to go where the money is. That's where you launch your boat.

You constantly reassess during the day. I'll also evaluate the SOX—the Philadelphia Semiconductor Sector Index. If I see strength in the SOX, then when S&P futures turn up I'm going to get long chip stocks.

Do you ever take a trading position home overnight?

All the time.

Many day traders won't venture into that Great Unknown. Overnights scare them, even if being right can bring hefty gains on a trade when the market opens. Why do you take the risk? Do you know more than anyone else?

I think that over the long term you get good at taking home overnights. I make money on them. But every once in a while you do get whacked. Maybe everybody else will make a few thousand dollars for the day, but you've lost $15,000 because you got whacked on your overnight.

When they hurt you, it's usually in the morning. You come in at 9:30 when the market opens. Let say I have a $5000 profit because I took home six different stocks. I want to preserve that, so I'm looking to close my overnights real quick and not let the market take all my profit away by 9:33, which has happened to me several times. So I'm not able to sit and watch the market, saying this is hot, this is moving. To me that's the biggest penalty for overnight. Plus, it can clog your head if you come in down $10,000 or $12,000.

So in the time you ordinarily would spend catching a market move or at least assessing the market's direction, you're just trying to cover your overnight positions. As you suggest, that's an enormous distraction—like trying to simultaneously watch a trading account and an investment account.

As a rule, you can make good money trading overnights. And once I lock in a profit, I go on with the day. Though if something has worked great and starts to move, I'm going to try and ride it for two or three bucks if it's taking off. Conversely, if I take home positions and they open down, I'll give them time to come back. I won't just sell out of them; I'll wait for some type of rally. For instance, if I go home short Amazon.com and the next morning it opens up, I'm not just going to cover immediately. I'm going to see if the move is real or if it's just opening hype.

What do you think about taking a trading position home over the weekend?

That's different. Sentiment can change. Enthusiasm that was there on Friday may have evaporated by Monday morning. I don't want that risk. In general, over a weekend, I usually don't take home more than a position or two.

A day trader obviously must have a good handle on risk. There's no shoulder you can cry on if you fail. And it does no good to scream at your computer. You're on your own. Earlier you mentioned discipline, instinct, and seasoned judgment as key to successful trading. Some traders operate more on instinct; others build a solid base of discipline. But what is seasoned judgment?

I don't know if it's distinct from discipline and instinct, or a combination of the two. It would be like if I've had a few bad days, I'll want to go home flat. I really don't want to go home long Amazon, but if the stock was out of control today it presents a good risk/reward. I've seen Amazon's pattern on the charts; I know it. That's instinct, but you use discipline to control yourself. So if I shouldn't take four [thousand shares] home, maybe I'll take two. Or if Amazon sold off hard, then rallied back six bucks, I'm going to short it and let it run $2 against me because I've seen that pattern before.

Seasoned judgment is applying discipline to what you are feeling. Discipline is saying I've had two losing days in a row, I didn't trade well, I'm going home flat, and I'm coming in with a clear head tomorrow. Seasoned judgment is I've lost $2000, the stock is not going my way, my instincts are that it's going to go my way, but let's close it out for now because I don't want to screw up my day betting against the stock. Even though I think I'm right, I have two choices: average down or close it out. Sometimes I don't want to go against the stock and have a losing day because I was wrong on one trade and let it kill me, even though I think I'm right.

I think you hit the nail when you said that seasoned judgment is discipline applied to your feelings.

I guess it is a combination of the two. You can have totally disciplined traders who don't let instinct get involved, and you can have totally instinctive traders who don't let discipline get involved. But both of those qualities over time grow into something better. When you have discipline and instinct in check, seasoned judgment grows.

In what ways have you become a better trader? Perhaps you have a recent example of a trade that went bad—a mistake you were able to correct that would have destroyed you in the beginning.

I did something really stupid with a stock called Applied Graphics. It gapped up 4 one morning. It had been down 10 the day before. I'd seen it gap up before and thought it wouldn't hold. I hit a $36 bid to short it immediately. Didn't even look at the news. Then I said to my partner, Brad, what's the story? He says Applied Graphics said they would miss their quarter by 4¢ but it's a one-time thing. That's pretty damned fundamental news. But by then, the stock was up to $38¼. I had shorted at $36. I'm already down $2250. It runs to $40. I'm down $4 on the stock because I haven't covered and I'm thinking, that was so stupid. It gets to $39½ on the bid and I shorted another one at $39½. I don't know why. It seemed right. I've seen these moves before—a company comes out and tries to talk their stock price up. It usually doesn't have much of an effect.

Now I'm 2000 short. One at $36, one at $39½. The stock is $39½ to $40¾. Then it started to turn down. The one I shorted at $39½ I covered at $37⅜ and made $2125 on that trade. The stock kept ticking down. I covered the second one at $35⅛, so I made money on that. And then I figured it had pulled back too far, so I got long at $35⅛ and made $1750 before it closed at $36¼. I was on the right side of the stock. I let it run $5 against me and I doubled up on my position. That's not preached in any books.

If you were just starting out as a trader and faced a similar choice, what might have happened?

I would have shorted the rally up higher and not taken so much risk. If you lost a half buck, you lost a half buck. A new person would have done better to buy the opening and take a quick buck out because it was running. What I did was turn a bad trade into a good trade. My first trade was bad because I didn't have the information I should have had to make that decision. A better trade would have been to watch it run up and then short two when it got up near $39 if you didn't think that level was going to hold. A new guy would see it moving quickly in the morning and try to jump in it long and take $1 out of it, or maybe after it ran three or four bucks to short it. Maybe he'd know the chart on it and say there is some resistance in this $40 area. It's not going above that. I look at charts for support and resistance levels to some degree, and new traders should definitely do that.

Does seeing the resistance levels in a stock require special insight, or are these movements fairly evident?

They're pretty straightforward. But they don't work in extreme situations. If there is huge buying in the stock, it will go right through resistance levels. If there is huge selling in the stock, you'll probably break support levels. But day to day, if the stock is up $4 it's probably not going to go up $6 if there is resistance at $4. So maybe I'd look to short there. If I'm wrong, I lose maybe a half buck. But if I'm right I'll probably get paid

$2. It's going to pull back from that level, it's not going to sit there. When I use charting for day trading, I want to be paid when I'm right. I'm not just going to try to take ⅜ and say, "Wow, I'm glad I used my chart." Because now the stock is down $3½ and I got only ⅜.

With the charts giving you confidence, you can move away from basic tick trading—settling for fractional gains—and hunt for bigger game.

Whenever I use charts. Depending on the market, I go between being a position trader and tick trading. This week, I thought the market was tough. On Monday I made money but not much; Tuesday I lost. Wednesday I became a tick trader. I shorted rallies, bought pullbacks. I didn't do anything too extreme.

You can make $1000 a day or more as a tick trader.

Yes, it is realistic for a good tick trader to make $1000 in a day. New people coming in should be tick traders until they develop more judgment. Not following that rule is why I got hurt so bad when I started. Brad and I were trading in my house by ourselves, and we competed to see who lost less in a day. It was a miserable point in both of our lives. We just went in there day after day and lost money. It was our mistake. It's imperative for new people to be around other successful traders. We were told you've got to trade around people who are making money. We would have saved ourselves a lot of grief had we done that.

Trade in groups? What happened to that fierce indepen-dence? Don't you in effect sell yourself short when other people are hovering about with opinions, habits, and maybe an ear for your profitable trades?

You need to be around people's ideas, people talking, people saying, "That's real stupid." If somebody is shorting Amazon when it's up $4 and I'm long two, I might say, "Why are you doing that?" I'm not going to tell him to get out of it. He may be right, and I may be wrong. If he's doing it because he thinks it's up enough, that's okay. But if he ends up losing a couple of bucks on it, I'm going to tell him that the market was too strong, the Internets were too strong, and he was fighting the tape. The reason I was long is because I didn't see a lot of people calling their brokers to sell Amazon quick because it's up $4.

The fact that you didn't see sellers rushing out of Amazon.com was a clue to the stock's underlying strength. In the same vein, a lack of buyers in a down stock is a sign of relative weakness. At these times, do you simply follow the crowd?

I'm always trying to think about what the public sitting at home would be doing. I think, if somebody owns this stock long, would they be calling today to sell it and take profits or put on a short? If my answer is no, maybe I want to stay long. If the answer is yes, then I want to stay short.

When you add a new stock to your universe, do you study it before you trade it or do you simply begin trading in an attempt to learn about it?

I usually pick up a new stock off the leader board and put it on my ticker. I'll pull up news for the day, pull up a chart on it, and also find out what the company does. I'll read a paragraph about the business and glance at revenues and earnings. I trade a stock a lot better if I know something about it. Some guys trade stocks all day and don't know them from anything. When I know something, I feel that maybe I have more of a right to trade.

So before you put a dime into any trade, you'll become familiar with at least the basics of a company. How much time do you give for that homework?

Five minutes. I know enough industries, enough companies, that I'm going to know what industry they are in and which is their top competition. I'm doing some quick and dirty charting, and I'm pulling up a paragraph on the company. It's imprecise, but it gives me more of a comfort level.

Does your research, as cursory as it is, ever steer you away from a trade because you don't like what you see?

Let's say a stock is up $3. I've never heard of it before. But it's on the leader board, so put it on my ticker and chart it. I see it really never goes up more than $3, and there is no volume behind this move. It's probably B.S. That would probably keep me out of it.

If I didn't know that, I may go for it and end up losing a quick buck. And if the chart has wild moves and the stock starts to run up again, I'm probably going to get long. If the stock has had $8 up days in the past, that says it can happen in the future. But unless I really like the fundamental news, I'm probably not going to be chasing it. The market is full of one-day wonders. It's up $3, it's going to be up $8 by the end of the day. It probably is not going to do squat for a long time thereafter.

Sometimes, though, I do want to get money out of these stocks. But you've got to decide if it's worth what you're trying to make. There's nothing worse than playing Amazon.com and making ¼ or ⅜ and it goes up another 3 points. Because every time you play, you're risking $1 on the spread alone. The bids are thin; they disappear. And unless you're incredibly quick, somebody may beat you to the punch. You've got to look at your risk/reward. You don't want to risk $2 to make ⅜. I've seen traders do that, and I laugh at myself when I do it. What was I trying to accomplish, and what kind of risk did I take?

Are there occasions when you might spend more than a few minutes with a stock before trading it?

Yes. If you're adding a staple to your ticker. A stock you want to trade for a while, you definitely want to put it on the ticker and watch it.

And when you're considering a potential addition to your core group, how long should you watch its trading patterns?

Watch it until you feel like you have a reason to buy it. You can't put a time limit on that. It might be a day or it might be two weeks.

We've talked a great deal about buying. How do you know when to sell? Before you initiate a trade, do you have a price target in mind or a certain amount of profit you want to pocket?

That really comes down to feel and to what the market is doing. I use the S&P 500 futures a lot. I look at the NASDAQ averages and the Dow, trying to get a feel for relative strength. Also, I'm looking at stocks that, for the most part, I have watched for a long time. I have a feel for how much they can go up and down, and what is a normal range.

Sapient (SAPE), a software company, is an example. I bought it one morning, made $1000 on it, and closed it. I didn't have a great sense of where it was going. But right around noon I saw the stock was up 6 points. I've traded SAPE for a couple years and I know $6 is too big a move. So I got short ¼ point off the top, held it, and made $1¾ on the downside. I wouldn't short Amazon.com because it was up $6. I would short SAPE if it was up that much because that's an abnormal move for the stock. To me, that was a smart play. The stock would have to go up $7 to really hurt me, and I was willing to give the stock $1000 against me.

How did the stock close that day?

I shorted it $50⅞, covered at $49⅛, and it closed at $48. Up $3½.

So you might have nearly doubled your gain had you held the trade longer.

I would have made more, but it comes down to being right versus being greedy.

If a buddy asked you for advice about day trading—he wanted to know your secrets and follow your lead—what would you say?

Tell me about the buddy.

He wants to be a successful trader. And you think he can do it.

Okay. That's one type of buddy.

What's another type of buddy?

The other type of buddy is the guy who has three kids and has to have a certain amount of money each month. I couldn't encourage him to take the risk.

You wouldn't encourage someone with a family and a mortgage to try his hand at day trading?

I wouldn't. If he wanted to do it, I would help him out as best I could. But I would almost go recruit Buddy A. I would feel guilty recruiting Buddy B.

Forget about recruiting; you're off the hook. These friends show up at your office, plant themselves in front of your computer, and they won't leave until you tell them everything you know. What's the first thing you say?

Play the action. You're never going to get any good if you're not playing the action. I'm not saying you want to come in and trade Amazon.com. Wait a couple of months before doing that. But you need to be with what's moving.

From the get-go, start out small. Start out with a 200-share lot and lose $400 or $500 or $1000 a day for a while. You'll be saying, "That was stupid. Why did I do that?" That's okay; you're getting experience. I would want them to trade small, play the action, listen well, and follow. If I'm making money in a stock, you probably want to follow me. If my partner Brad is printing money and I'm cussing, you probably want to be following Brad. Then give it six to nine months.

Playing the action sounds a bit scary. Maybe the action is too much, too fast.

There are two types of traders. They are, by nature, either instinctive or disciplined. If discipline is their nature and they are conservative, they need to play the action and take more risk, because this is a risk-taking game. If they are on the instinct side like I was, they'll need more discipline. Me, I couldn't wait to beat my chest. I threw away $6000 during lunch—and you shouldn't be trading around lunch.

Why not trade during lunch?

The major moves in the market are before 11:30 A.M. and after 1:30 P.M. I do trade during lunch, but I don't trade a major trend. I'm just scalping a quarter here and there. Around lunchtime the market makers have less order flow. And when they have fewer orders, they can trade more effectively against us.

Since NASDAQ market makers don't process as many orders during lunchtime, they can take aim at day traders. It's kind of a sport.

Yeah, and they're all good traders. They try to take advantage of us or beat us during the lunch hours. They can't do it when there is big order flow. What can they do if we're buying in, riding the coattails up, or they've got big sellers and we're short in the stock? They might know that some day trader just shorted 3000 shares, but they've got a huge sell order coming in. They can't really try to run out the short first.

Trading volume is strong in the morning, troughs during lunch, and builds again in the afternoon toward the close. What's the best strategy during lunchtime to beat a market maker at his own game?

The best trade at lunch is to take the opposite side of any action that seems too extreme for the lunch hour. The price moves are probably not as extreme as the market makers are taking it. Traders have loaded up long on a stock, and though the market makers don't have many buy or sell orders, they know a lot of people are long. So they'll take it down two points when they should have only taken it down one, just to rough people up. If I see that stock down $2, and I don't think it's a real move, I'll try to get on the bid and buy it, ride it up, and take a quick half buck out of it.

Still, day traders, with their ability to make markets and move stocks, are effectively forcing professional market makers to share or even forfeit a stock's bid and ask spread. That's hardly going to endear you to them. Won't market makers try to derail day traders at every turn?

When they have to worry about buying or selling 100,000 shares, they can't worry about five day traders. Market makers are good traders. They each trade a couple of dozen stocks. If they could trade one stock like we do, and they didn't have huge order flow one way, they would probably beat us. It would be hard to make money because the table would be tilted in their favor. But when there is heavy order flow, there's nothing they can do.

Yet the market makers are not simply going to hand you money.

They do know the market. And particularly in a stock with light volume, they will try to beat the day traders if they can. Suppose news flashes on CNBC about a thinly traded stock. Immediately 15 day traders buy it. It's lunchtime. The market makers really don't have much order flow. Those day traders are trying to make a quick ⅛ or ¼. The market makers lift the bid; people are trading the stock up. A few guys get out quick and make ¼ or ⅜ of a point. But the market makers are all short in the stock now. They don't have order flow coming in. Where can the stock go? Back to the level it was at before the announcement.

But what the market makers will do is take the stock down further than it was before the positive announcement, just to run us out. We'll be trying to get out of positions and they're making us pay. They're not trying to devise ways to beat us, but they certainly don't want us to take advantage of them either. So if they've got you trapped on the wrong side of a trade, they'll try to run you out. This is where seasoned judgment can make a difference. The disciplined trader will likely bail out early while the seasoned trader will bid for stock as the weak hands sell out. The seasoned trader will recognize the market makers' true intentions.

Brad Frericks
Play the Action

"You've got to limit your losses to stay in the game."

A few years and one lifetime ago, Brad Frericks put his certified public accountant training to work as a controller for a tiny savings and loan in Elmhurst, Illinois, just outside of Chicago. The office days were rather uneventful until the company announced it would convert from a depositor-owned thrift to public ownership. As a reward for their support, depositors received shares of the initial public offering. And in what was then a bull market for financial companies, the little thrift's stock price made a big jump in its first days of trading.

Frericks soon noticed many other thrifts completing identical conversions with similar upside results to their stock prices. So he teamed up with Jim Shaw, a high school friend from his hometown of Quincy, Illinois, in an attempt to capitalize on this growing trend.

The pair had a simple plan: open deposit accounts at dozens of these mutual thrifts around the country and flip the

IPO shares for a quick score. The pickings were good for a while as larger numbers of thrifts did choose to go public. But when too many people discovered the money that could be made, the opportunities were soon arbitraged away.

Frericks went looking for other ways to participate in the equity market without becoming a stockbroker. In 1996, he and Shaw became involved with day trading. By then, the partners had moved to Atlanta, where they started buying and selling stocks through an electronic trading system they had installed at Shaw's house.

Flipping thrift IPOs proved far more satisfying than their new gamble. The beginning months were torturous and money-losing, and trying to trade without more experienced hands around only exacerbated the pain. But they stuck it out. Frericks didn't know it at the time, but in fact he was ahead of the curve in one important way. His instincts about mutual thrift conversions had been right on the money, and the experience had taught him a key insight of successful traders: *play the action, and whenever possible, come early to the game.*

Frericks, 35, and day traders like him hope to find the spot where a crowd will form—before it actually does. But how? Day traders face that thorny question with each opening bell. The answer is one of the tricks of the trade.

■   ■   ■

Day traders often use various mental and physical exercises to gear up for the task ahead. What's a key tool that helps put you in the right frame of mind for trading?

I go to the gym at 6:30 A.M., work out, and read *Investors' Business Daily* (IBD). I study the page with the previous day's NASDAQ winners and the losers, and I look at their volume.

You watch volume, as in the number of shares traded. What's so important about that?

Volume tells me the stock's relative strength. Are people interested in buying or selling? If normally a stock does 100,000 shares a day, but yesterday it did 500,000 shares, I want to know why. I'm always looking for a change in direction of a stock, because that's going to change my position. If there's no volume, there's really no change.

Where's the value in yesterday's share volume? People don't make money trading old news.

I want to see how the stock opens. If the stock follows through and opens strong, I want to buy it on the first pullback. I use IBD and volume charts to see what's hot, and a lot of those stocks get put on my ticker. I'm constantly checking throughout the day to find new prospects to trade. If a stock is up $5 on Monday, I want to watch it on Tuesday. It might give back a dollar in a strong market, and then on Wednesday it's sitting around. But say on Thursday morning I notice that it's got some volume and it's up a dollar, I might give it a whirl. It's on my screen because for some reason it was up $5 on Monday on good volume, and I will follow that stock sometimes for the next couple of weeks. I might not notice every tick, but I pay attention if volume picks up. Then I say, "That stock is on my ticker for a reason," and I'll trade it.

For example, not long ago I traded a software company called Aspect Development—symbol ASDV—a small-capitalization stock. I noticed that its competitors were getting hammered, and Aspect Development was the only stock in the group that hadn't been getting beat up. I'm thinking that in the near term, this stock has to be weak, since the whole industry is. So I shorted it anytime it made a run. I would watch the volume and try to dominate the stock—trading 5000 shares at a time if I could. Throughout the day I would focus on that stock and four or five others.

Is it your trading style to move quickly in and out for pocket change—quarters and half-dollars—or do you like to give your picks some room to run?

I probably do 70 trades a day—about 70,000 shares. I'm typically not a tick trader, trying to capture ⅛ or ¼. I don't go into a trade trying to make $125 or $250. If I think I'm right on a trade, I'll try to ride it for a little bit more.

A good trader has to uncover clues about a stock in not-so-obvious places. Stocks with heavy volume get your attention. But how do you decide which of the lot to drive home?

I have an accounting background, so I focus on fundamentals. We do a lot of technical charting, looking for breakouts to the upside and the downside. I know where a stock like Aspect Development has been for the past week. I pull up a chart to see where it's been in the past six months and where the 50-day moving average is. I don't do intraday charting, but I do want to know the volume it's done every day. And you develop a memory for all that. Memory is a big part of the game. When the market is up 250 points, memory doesn't matter. It's who can hit the keyboard the fastest. But in a normal trading range, memory serves you well about where the stock has been.

By looking at charts, I know the history of the stock and what it normally does in volume. I want to know if the market maker has some big client who's trying to accumulate a short position. Either the short is going to get blown out of the water or it's right. I'm going to take a chance that somebody is accumulating a short position which will keep selling pressure on the stock. I look at the chart and see where the stock has formed a strong base. If it breaks through that on the downside, I'm going to stay with my short.

Fundamental analysis in day trading seems oxymoronic. Do you really care about investment criteria like earnings per share? After all, this is buy and sell, not buy and hold.

Fundamental analysis actually has hurt me. People have made a lot of money trading the Internets, and I was slow to jump on board. I just didn't believe it. I might be a little bit different than others for that reason, but I didn't understand their strength at the time. People in 1998 were buying what they heard about and what was strong. They didn't care about value.

Some of these Internet plays are more difficult to trade than so-called market stocks like Intel and Dell Computer. There aren't as many shares outstanding, and these stocks carry wider bid and ask spreads. If you can buy on the bid and sell at the offer, capturing that spread will bank a tidy profit. But the risk is exponentially greater if the stock moves against you. Given the downside, what other reasons motivate you and other day traders to venture into stocks with big spreads?

I don't want to give the secret away. Trading stocks with big spreads has a couple of advantages. If I think I know the direction of the stock, I can go in between the bid and the ask and narrow the gap. Also, these stocks are not played by everyone. Many day traders are not even familiar with them, which is nice. But with a stock like Yahoo!, everybody is there. Day traders drive the market for the stock.

You can tell when successful traders are playing these wide-spread stocks. They're not afraid to lose $1500 or $2000 on a trade. They'll whack at the offer, hit the bid, and take a chance. If I like a stock, I'm not afraid to pay the offer on a stock with a $1.50 or $2 spread and see what happens. Because with a big spread between the bid and the ask, I can read the market makers much easier, and there aren't so many people involved. I feel I know what I'm in for. When I make the trade, I know exactly from the market maker's reaction if I'm going to win or lose.

Why is it easier to read the market makers in a stock with a big spread?

Because it's a low-volume stock. When you buy 1000 shares or short 1000 shares of a low-volume stock, you can tell the impact immediately. It makes it easier to read the stock when your 1000 shares make a difference. If the market makers don't have a buy or sell order, either they're going to get out of the way and lift a level, or they have more of an agenda—they've got somebody trying to accumulate a large position, for instance. In either case, you have a better idea of what they're up to.

Eventually you get to know how a stock trades and which market makers dominate it. If you trade Yahoo! or Dell Computer or Microsoft, you can't tell what's going on with the other traders' positions. Here, I'm reading the market makers to see what they do and watching the trading volume in the stock. One particular market maker, for instance, is famous for going high bid on a stock, acting like he has lots of stock to buy, when in fact he's a seller, and by 11 A.M. he's sitting on the offer and won't go anywhere.

So there are clear advantages to trading large-spread, low-volume stocks, especially not having a lot of people around you competing for the same buck. But that seems like an edge that develops only for sophisticated traders.

Right. Someone who starts out day trading should play the ⅛- or teenie-spread stocks until they get used to day trading and to what market makers and volume do to a stock. They'll go broke fast if they start playing stocks with unusually wide spreads.

Still, the trade-off in a thinly traded stock is that rival traders and market makers know exactly what you're doing. It's not like losing yourself in a big crowd of Intel traders.

That makes it more fun, because I don't exactly know what the market makers know. They're trying to get a sense of who's short and who's long. It's a big cat-and-mouse game. My favorite part of electronic trading is reading the market makers. Those guys come to play. We used to blow them off and buy or sell them out of the way. Now you do that and you could be in serious trouble.

Are there any particular stocks or industries that traders should focus on first, or is it best just to play the action?

Playing the action is what it's all about. If they are just starting out trying to trade, they might look at Dell, for instance. Everybody will tell you not to trade Dell, because market makers have their best people on it and you're going to get blasted. But you have to trade Dell, Yahoo!, Cisco Systems, and a few other stocks with narrow spreads. You can get out without losing a lot of money and learn what a powerful stock is all about. Then you want to find a stock like Aspect Development, which typically has a wider spread, so you can learn how to trade those.

The "action" stocks are not necessarily the most active. I don't necessarily mean Dell or Microsoft—you get the same most-actives all the time. I'm talking about the most active stocks relative to what they normally do in share volume. That takes a little learning. But then you'll see a stock like Aspect Development and understand why it's doing 250,000 shares today when normally it does 50,000. You'll see that a lot if you scan the market for stocks that are in play.

What key point about trading do you know now that you wish someone had told you in the beginning?

When I started, it was just my partner and me. Neither of us was experienced at trading, and we tried to trade out of his house. The biggest mistake day traders make is trying to trade out of their homes, by themselves, without proper training and other information. There is a lot to be said for being in a room with more people than just you. That was the first mistake I made—not becoming involved in a group or trading with other people. Trading in a group can be really helpful provided that you can find a group that knows what they are doing.

You chide yourself for trading at home, but what's wrong about being the lone wolf? After all, with day trading,

every day is Independence Day. It's just you and the computer, so why do you need a support group?

Mainly because there are just more ideas available. I know more about some stocks and you know more about others. When I come into the office, the chitchat in the morning goes something like this: "Why is this stock bid up?" "Anybody hear any news?" "What did you read about?" "This stock is breaking out of the charts." There are just so many more stocks to play because of ideas from people in the office.

Trading around other people also gives you confidence in what you're doing. If the other people in the room can do it, you can do it. You realize what works and what doesn't in a particular market. Nowadays I could stay at home and trade and make a good living. Yet an office environment with quality traders benefits me a lot, and I think I make more money than I would staying at home.

Speaking of money, how much initial capital do you think someone needs to start day trading in a meaningful way?

Start with $75,000 or $100,000 at the most. You don't want too much because you don't want to have the ability to lose a lot. Yet you want to be able to buy 1000 shares of a stock and with leverage also trade two or three other stocks at a time. If you have only $20,000 in the account and the market soars, you're going to feel like you missed out. More than that, it's going to shoot your confidence when you see everybody around you making money, and here you are trading with $20,000.

Is there a difference between the day trading that you practice and the trading that someone does through an

online brokerage? If an Internet trader buys a stock at the open and sells it $1 higher at the close, isn't that person also an electronic day trader? Or are your motivations so different?

If I buy Aspect Development and it goes up $3, it's hard for me not to take the profit. I'm sure day traders sitting at home are feeling the same—if they are day traders. The way to discern between day traders and investors is whether they're going to say, "I'm not taking that $3 on Aspect Development; I know it's going up $10." They're going to give it a week.

Pure day traders are taking profits all the time. They're not keeping a position for a week. If I want to do that, I'll call my broker. If a stock is giving me a couple points a day, I'm out of there and on to the next trade. If I see more upside in that same stock, I'll get back in. That's the difference between the pure day trader and the guy online with E*Trade or Charles Schwab. A lot of people are day trading, but they don't have the information or the speed. They're not in and out, which makes sense. They'd be totally at a disadvantage.

How are these armchair day traders at a disadvantage? Through the Internet, they also have access to real-time information and quotes.

By the time they pick up the phone or log on and place their order on the Internet, guys like me can buy or sell 10,000 shares of the stock they're in. When they're still calling to see if their order got filled, the trade's gone and I've already made $500 or $1000. So they're at a disadvantage both in terms of speed and in seeing what the market makers are doing. People like that are better off with week-long trades.

Day trading really owes its popularity to the Internet, which made it possible for anyone with a modem and a mouse to master the fine art of stock market speculation. Which way do you see the business heading? Are we going to look back in 10 years at one of the greatest bull markets of the twentieth century and wonder whatever happened to this determined band of electronic traders who were able to move markets?

Sometimes I'm afraid that the whole thing is just going to blow up and a lot of people are going to get hurt, and they're going to have to change something. Day trading controls the NASDAQ right now. Overall, I think the stock market is the best place to be as far as investing, and if the majority of the population wants to become involved and have the best technology to trade it, so be it. Everyone has the ability to get on the Internet. They're going to get better opportunities, and pretty soon they're going to be just as fast as us and have the same information. I think that's the way it should be.

But if people trade on the same information as you, doesn't that eliminate your edge? One of the inside tracks that professional day traders have over less experienced traders—in fact, the main line—is access to better and faster information. If that playing field is leveled and day trading becomes more efficient, your advantage disappears.

The strong will survive. There are no punches pulled here. The majority of people who try to day trade fail. The percentage who survive will probably go down because of competition. It won't hurt people like me. Competition will disadvantage new people. But it's going to make better traders of those who have experience and know how to adapt to the changes.

You're quite confident about day trading's future. What would be the first bit of advice you would tell someone just coming into the profession?

Know where the action is. Try to find the 10 stocks with the most action for that day. If you sit long enough in front of the screen and you're on top of the 10 stocks with the most action, whether they're going up or down, you're going to make money in the long run after you learn how to trade them.

To make money in the action stocks—or any stock you trade, for that matter—it helps to know some of the stock's trading history.

Right. Know a bit of the stock's history, and swing the bat. Give it a whirl. That's the only way to learn. Start small. The money you make will be small at first, but you also won't lose as much. When I started, I lost a little every day. It gnawed on me. I can't to this day tell you what caused it to turn around, except I began to recognize what the hot stocks were, what the volume was on a stock, and why it was acting the way it was. Then I started trading smaller lots and I got in and out more often. *You've got to limit your losses to stay in the game. Longevity is key here. The longer you can stay in it, the more money you can make.*

Do you see electronic day trading as a long-term career for people, or is it a short-term affair—rather like your relationship with the stocks you buy and sell? Maybe it's

the constant action and the unrelenting intensity, but day trading seems mostly a young person's profession.

It really is a young person's game. It's hard work to sit in front of the screen all the time, every day. I can't pass up the money because it's so good and I feel like I'm just coming into my own, so I'm going to do it until something else comes along. But it's definitely not a "put in 30 years, take your pension, and retire" line of work.

What I do now is stay in front of the screen every minute of the trading day. Now and then I go to lunch. But my profit and loss statement is staring me in the face. It forces you to come to terms with yourself or it's going to drive you crazy. I'm getting better at being away from the market, but when you have so much information on the market all the time, it's hard to get away completely. That's one bad thing about day trading. My partner and I find that we're always talking about stocks. Maybe that's the fault of everyone and their jobs, but I think with day trading you are so intense, with so much information, that you probably shouldn't do it for a long period.

Day traders aren't going to be doing this for 30 years anyway, because in a short time they've made more money than most people do, and they're going to move on to bigger things and different types of trading. Pure day trading, sitting in front of the screen, for all those reasons is something you do for maybe 10 years. You either grow out of it, or you don't make any money and you leave.

Jonathan Petak
Don't Fight the Tape

---

*"Everybody has good days in this business.
What matters is how well you control your losing days."*

S ome traders work days; others work nights—overnights, to be specific. But overnight trading is not sitting in front of a computer screen until dawn. Taking an overnight involves holding a long or short position after the market closes until it opens the following morning. But the overnight game, in every sense, is trading in the dark. In those few hours, anything can happen to individual companies or entire economies. Meanwhile, you're stuck on the wrong side of a trade with thousands of shares and no chance to unload them. Then the opening bell mercifully rings and the stock immediately runs a few points against you.

So it's easy to see how overnights can offer sizeable returns, but can also carry equally large risks. Executing these trades properly requires art and skill. Jonathan Petak has specialized in this arena for six years, and in that time he has developed a gutsy, unique style. As his palette, this 30-year-old trader uses the colorful, most active stocks on the New York

Stock Exchange—the "Big Board"—and the briskly traded shares on NASDAQ. And he favors a big canvas—typically holding 20,000 shares—and occasionally 50,000 shares—of a single stock.

At first sight, these mammoth gambits seem daunting and daredevilish, but Petak tempers them with strong measures of risk control. Above all, he doesn't fight the tape. He learned the hard way not to second-guess the trend in a stock. If a stock is strong, he buys. If it's weak, he shorts. Fewer surprises mean greater profits.

Petak also won't acquire a full position in one swoop. Instead, he builds a position carefully, typically buying or selling a few thousand shares at a time over the course of a trading day. Individual investors do much the same when they take a set amount of money and dollar-cost average into a stock or mutual fund each month, buying at different prices along the way. The major difference is that Petak is reluctant to add to positions going against him; however, he will aggressively add to positions moving in his favor.

Like all investment strategies, this one carries a trade-off between risk and reward. Stocks tend to make their largest moves at the opening. A good overnight may gap open several points, netting a handsome profit. On the other hand, a poor overnight may gap down sharply, leaving the trader with a large loss and little chance to undo the damage. But what other day traders may achieve in a good week, or an investor may achieve in months, Petak frequently achieves over a day and a night. That's yet another reason why trading and investing are as different as night and day.

■   ■   ■

What was your first experience with trading?

I was working for the consulting firm Ernst & Young as a computer programmer and had been put on a project at what was then Shearson Lehman Brothers. Every day during lunch I would hop up to the trading floor. I had always wanted to be a trader and I was trying to get a job, but they weren't offering. One day I just pounced into one of the vice presidents' offices. He was startled, but he did me a favor. He couldn't give me a job, but he knew someone who could. So he made a couple of telephone calls and I got a clerk position at a trading firm.

A clerk in a trading firm is not like being a trader, but at least you got close to the action.

My salary went from $2500 a month to $200 a week. I would get lunch and breakfast for everybody on the desk, read out their trades, do grunt work, and I was just miserable for six months. But I knew that I would get the opportunity to trade. I did, and thankfully it's been pretty good ever since.

What sort of trading were you exposed to at this firm?

Most of the traders there were doing overnights. They start getting into the market around 2:30 P.M. and hold positions overnight, the premise being that the stocks they're buying are closing on big volume and will open up strong the next day. Then they sell it at the open, and do the opposite if they're short. I started out doing that. I wasn't really allowed to day trade. I just took overnights and would spend the next day getting out of them. Finally they let me day trade.

Was there a particular reason you started out trading overnights?

I was on a desk where the head trader was an overnighter, and I was learning from him. At other desks the head traders were day traders. If I had been on their desk, maybe I would have started out day trading.

How does the risk of overnight trading compare to what you would face in day trading?

In day trading, your risk is only limited to a particular time frame, whereas taking home 20,000 IBM overnight, I don't know what could happen. They could announce something after the close or before the open and I might be out. The volatility is more extreme, as opposed to day trading where it's not so bad. Still, I find the risk of overnights is limited and overall I think the potential return is worth it, provided that the trades are done properly.

Overnights actually seem one of the riskiest trades of all. How can you claim that their risk is limited? In fact, one of the often-repeated day-trading rules is to control risk by not taking overnight positions.

With overnights, you're building a position throughout the day—we're not in and out. If you buy 5000 IBM at noon and you're up a half a point and then at 2 P.M. it's still acting well, you buy more. By the end of the day you have 20,000 shares and you're up a point on it. Taking that profit home overnight, you are really playing with the house's money. Consider that as opposed to buying 20,000 shares in one shot just before the market close. You have no profit in it.

Averaging into a position is a way to control risk?

Yes. I believe in building up a position in the stock, because then you're not so worried about what is going to happen that night. You sleep well. You have profit in there already. So if you take home 50,000 Intel and you're up two points on it, if it opens down two points then you're not losing—you're just giving back what you made yesterday. The thing about overnights is that it's easier to hit triples and home runs. With day trading it's more singles and doubles. The two keys to overnights are not to add to positions that aren't going your way and never to take home losing positions. If you follow these rules your chances for success are good.

How do you find stocks to play?

I'm trading relative strength. That's all. The market goes up, the stock doesn't go up, it's weak, and I short it. If we're down 200 points and you have stocks that don't go down, you've got to buy them. Don't fight the tape. If the market is selling off and Intel is up ½, I'm going to buy Intel.

You're buying and shorting throughout the day. Do you trade differently in the closing minutes than you would at other times?

Between 3:45 P.M. and 4 P.M., if the positions in my portfolio that I'm long don't break higher, or the ones that I'm short don't break lower, I won't add any more. I'm not going to get bigger because momentum isn't that strong. Frequently, I'll close out positions that I don't think warrant taking home.

So you've established all your positions going into the last 15 minutes of trading, unless there's enough momentum to warrant adding to your positions. And because you're only taking overnights when stocks are going away, you are only taking home positions when you have profits. But

there's still a chance that the stock will break against you in the morning.

It does happen that you get hurt. But again, I feel good because I am trading from strength and hopefully only risking my profits. I don't feel like I'm taking too much risk. When I am wrong, generally I only give back part of my profits, and when I am right I am a huge winner.

Now it's the following morning. The opening bell has rung, signaling the start of the trading day. What are you doing?

I'm looking to see what kind of opening we're having. If it's an up opening, I'm going to sell out of my longs. If it's a big down opening, I'm going to cover my shorts. I believe in the ABC wave. When the market has a big up opening, for example, the opening is the A wave. The B wave is going to come probably 5 or 10 minutes later, when the market pulls back. During the B wave I'm going to cover my shorts. I want to sell my longs when the market is going up and cover my shorts when the market is going down, which is the opposite of what the individual investor does. The individual investor will buy when the market is going up and sell when the market is going down.

What's the C wave?

The C wave comes at about 10 A.M. It's another move in the market and is usually a continuation of the direction of the opening move. All day the market is making waves. But I find you can really work off of the ABC wave in the morning.

Once you unwind the previous day's overnights, the process repeats itself. When do you start angling into a

trade, and how many shares are typically accumulated in that initial phase?

Sometimes beginning about 10 A.M. I'll build a position— 2000, 4000 shares—and go from there.

What's the biggest position you've ever held overnight?

I was long 50,000 Intel. It was breaking out of a pattern. The next day it was up $5. But I didn't make $5 a share. I was selling it little by little as it was going up. By the end of the day it was up $5. But it opened up about $2 and kept going higher, and every time it would go higher, I would sell some more. I made about three points on the stock.

What told you the stock was breaking out of a pattern and gave you the confidence to amass such a large number of shares?

It was trading on huge volume compared to what it usually does, which is something that I always look at. I won't touch stocks that have garbage volume. It had broken out of a nice base, the chart looked great, and all the characteristics were in play. It was what I call a "five-star overnight." I wanted to be big in it, and I felt really good about it.

How many shares does a more typical overnight trade involve?

Between 4000 and 20,000 shares.

After exiting that massive Intel trade, would you then reaccumulate the position in a huge way and hold it overnight again? You said the stock had broken out of a pattern.

No. I felt like that was the move. I'd take home like 4000 to 10,000 shares, but nothing big.

Which would you say dominates your trading—instinct or discipline?

I have a lot more instinct than discipline. I have a tendency to make a lot and then lose a lot, because my instincts are far superior to my discipline. I'd probably be up some ridiculous amount of money this year if I had better discipline. I'm working on it. I write in a journal every day, which I'm finding very helpful.

How does keeping a diary help your trading?

I sit for 10 minutes after the market close and talk to myself. I go over what I did right, what I did wrong. Sometimes I'll call myself an idiot and say I should have done this or that. Other times I'll tell myself, "Keep your head up; it's not so bad. You'll get them tomorrow." Positive things, sometimes negative things, but words that make me feel better.

Introspection and self-criticism about trading may take more confidence than the trades themselves.

You listen to yourself while you're writing. You don't just feel bad and complain. So maybe it gets stored more easily. The idea is to try and figure out what works and what doesn't work for you.

Do you reread the journal entries from time to time?

Yes. I like to read it on vacation to clear my thoughts and to remember what I was doing well and what I was doing poorly. I find it helps me to be more consistent.

So the personal journal is a form of self-tutoring? What are some lessons you've learned?

Trying to keep my losses to 10 percent of my month is a big lesson. So if I'm up 100 grand, the goal is not to lose more than 10 grand. Also, I have a tendency to fight the trend; don't fight the trend. Another lesson: ease in and ease out. And always get in small and get out small, taking it easy, not putting up a huge position all at once.

Successful trading is a convergence of timing, skill, instinct, and discipline. Some traders who have experienced this winning blend compare it to an athletic competition where every score, every defense, goes your way. Would you agree?

When I'm trading well, I feel like I'm in the zone. You just feel like everything you do is right. I can't even describe it. You're looking at your screen and it's like you have blinders on. Everything you touch is right. Your instincts are fantastic. Your feel is unbelievable. You know where the stocks are going. It doesn't happen all the time, but when it happens, you know it, and it's a tremendous high.

The "zone" sounds like a remarkable place to find yourself. How can a day trader discover the key to this zone?

The zone isn't someplace you try to go—it just happens. To get into the zone, you have to have a couple of good days before. They feed off each other and it's like a snowball effect. Your discipline is fantastic, you're cutting losses and making money every day, and you're hitting singles and doubles. Then, when you least expect it, you hit triples and home runs.

But although getting into the zone "just happens," as you say, don't you still have to point yourself in its direction?

For me, if the market has rhyme and reason—all the banks are up or all the technology stocks are down—then it's easier to get into the zone. I like to play groups, and if the groups are mixed—if you have six drug stocks on your screen and Pfizer and Merck are up, but Eli Lilly and Schering-Plough are down—I'm probably not going to trade the drugs because I couldn't tell from a hole in the wall what's going on there. Then there's no way you can get into the zone.

So if one favorite group is mixed, you switch to another.

I try to find another group and if I don't, then you've got to lay back and sit on your hands. *Everybody has good days in this business. What matters is how well you control your losing days.*

Suppose you've reached your monthly profit goal. It would seem that one of the best ways to control losses would be simply to stop trading.

If someone makes $50,000 in his first week and that's his goal for the month, then I believe he shouldn't hide the puck but keep trading and just be a little light. Trade smart, and cut down on size. If you meet your goal, that's a tremendous accomplishment and you should be commended, but at the same time you still want to stay in the game and make sure you don't miss a big day.

So you miss an opportunity. What's wrong with that?

Nothing. But if the day is great and you see other traders making money, then you want to get involved also. You just don't want to say, "I'm done." I believe in taking off when you're doing poorly. When you're doing well, you want to stay. You don't want to get out of your seat. That's the only time you're going to be able to press; you're not going to press when you're down. But you can trade smaller. Someone who has been trading 1000 shares can trade 300 shares.

After six years of trading, by now you know a few ropes. How long did it take for you to graduate to consistent winner from greenhorn trader?

The first two years I had to learn the rules and discovered that you have to get humble. You have to have big losing days before you can have your best winning days. The ones who don't get humble won't make it.

Maybe those traders are not humble because they rarely lose.

I don't know how many of those people there are.

Does anyone ever suffer losses and not get humble?

No. You're always going to get humble if you lose.

Some of those people no doubt are going to shut down their computers and walk away.

Then they got humble to the point where they didn't want to do it anymore. But I'm talking about people who are successful, who are still in the business. They've had their share of pitfalls.

What's been your worst trading day ever?

Once I shorted 10,000 shares of Alex Brown over the weekend—and it got taken over and was up 18 points on Monday.

Doing the quick math, that amounts to a $180,000 loss. And in a takeover play, it's a complete write-off. There's virtually no chance to get whole again. Did you want to quit?

No, but it was very depressing. That was the critical point of my trading. I realized that it's not how much you lose, it's how you bounce back. I knew that if I could bounce back from this, I could bounce back from anything.

Obviously, you've lived to tell the tale. How did you recover?

I had to trade smaller and ease into my stocks. And then every day I tried to make just a little bit. The big days were going to come, I had confidence, if I could just stick to what I did best.

The typical reaction after such a terrific beating would be to take more aggressive shots.

Yes, but traders who make it know to get small when decisions are not going well. Those who get bigger when they're losing eventually blow up.

What got you embedded in the Alex Brown trade in the first place?

I was fighting the tape. The stock was up all day. I should have never taken it home. On Friday it was acting great and there was a takeover rumor going around. I thought, this is bull, and I kept shorting it. My roommate worked at Alex Brown. He said that there's no way; the top officials are on the golf course. Little did I know that all these deals happen on the golf course. So Monday morning I picked up *The Wall Street Journal* and saw it right there.

Did your bosses know the extent of this position when you left work that Friday?

I'm not sure that they were aware of it until Monday. Then one of the head guys said, "Get out of all your stocks and take the day off." I got out of all my stocks. It was a horrible day.

So you were told not to trade and to pack it up for the day. Did you think they'd fire you?

No. I wasn't afraid I was going to be fired. I think it's all part of trading. I did some stupid things, but they had confidence in me. You're not going to let one day affect your trading career. It was important that I took a day off. It gave me an opportunity to think about my mistakes.

After the Alex Brown experience, do you think twice before shorting stocks that are rallying on takeover or other rumors?

If I see that happening again, I won't go near it. If there is a rumor that a stock might be taken over, I'll go with the trend and buy it. I won't fight it, meaning short it. With Alex Brown I was fighting the trend; that's why I took a loss. Alex Brown was closing at its high on big volume, and there was a rumor going around. I could have bought it and I would have made a whole lot of money.

So you'll stay away from the rumors on the short side. No Monday morning surprises for you.

Right. These things often happen over the weekend.

Do you read the business press?

I read *Business Week* and the *Journal* once in a while, but it clouds my judgment. I don't like to have any opinions. I just want to trade the stocks the way they are telling me to trade them. If the stock is strong and 20 people in the paper say the stock is going down, I don't want to be biased and short it. Some people could read the paper and not let those opinions affect them. I'm not strong enough.

Usually, market makers—not takeovers—determine the going price of a stock. But unlike the NASDAQ, bid and ask spreads for New York Stock Exchange–listed stocks are set by individuals known as "specialists." What have you learned about these exchange-floor traders?

Some specialists have their own schtick. And sometimes you will get screwed. You'll go to buy IBM, for instance. It will say $128 by $128¼, and the specialist will fill you at $128½. He can do that. There can be up to a two-minute lag time between when you put your order in and when he makes the decision to give you stock. Specialists can be more fair at certain times than others.

But these Big Board stocks are bellwethers, and you're trading thousands of shares at a time. You'd think the spreads would be more consistent.

In October 1997, when we were down a few hundred points and then bounced back the next day, you should have seen what was going on. These NYSE specialists were putting stocks a point wide. They made a fortune that day. Some day traders made a lot of money, too, but not like those guys. Then again, some of the specialists got really hammered the day before when they were forced to buy stocks all the way down.

Given the specialists' involvement, do you trade NYSE-listed stocks differently than NASDAQ stocks?

I don't get caught up with the specialists. As far as I'm concerned, if the stock is strong, there is nothing the specialist can do. If there are buyers, he's got to sell them stock. The way that I was taught is really the only way I've seen that is successful with the listed stocks—trading relative strength and relative weakness.

That said, some stocks on the over-the-counter market are easier to trade. Intel or Microsoft are more liquid than IBM or Texas Instruments. They are thicker and have huge volumes. You're not going to get hung by the specialists. If Intel is trading $86 by $86 and a teenie, I will get $86 and a teenie, no problem. It's all computerized.

What are some other ways people trade listed stocks?

A lot of people are really technical. I've never really seen traders who are technical be consistently successful. They get caught up in all the charts. I don't like to get too involved in charts, although I like to see that the trend is still intact.

With the big blocks you're trading, can you individually impact the price of a stock?

No, because the stocks I trade size in are very thick. Intel trades 25 million shares on some days.

Why not take large positions in more illiquid stocks?

It's not worth the risk. If I get caught and go to sell the stock, the stock would go down four or five points. We have stocks that we refer to as half-share stocks and full-share stocks. The half-share stocks are illiquid, with big spreads.

What's a big spread, in your estimation?

A ½ or ¾ point, as opposed to the ⅛ or teenie of an Intel. With Intel, you can trade big and won't have a hard time getting out. Intel trades nice and slow. The Internet stocks are not illiquid, but they trade thin. They're crazy. You could get hurt. You can't get out of a 50,000 share-lot as fast. I would never trade that size in those Internet stocks. I trade them small— 2000, 4000 shares. On those stocks I'm looking to make ¾ to a point on a trade. The more volatile the stock, the more profit you look for. But at the same time you're trading them smaller, so you can give them more room on the downside.

There must be a proven way to beat the specialists at their own game.

The way to beat the specialists is by having great timing for the waves in the market. You have to learn to anticipate the bounces and sell-offs. If the S&P futures are coming down, but the overall trend is strong, you want to buy. Always buy into weakness and sell into strength. And the key to when you buy is to start seeing when the move is over on the downside. You don't have to catch the bottom. You'll see people starting to buy at one level, and you'll buy at a higher point. But your timing is still a lot better than the next guy's. If you do the opposite, the specialist is going to get you. Still, you learn to live with your losing days, because everyone is going to have them. Once you are able to realize that you will lose money, you can find nirvana with this job.

The Trader's Edge

O ur first book, *The Electronic Day Trader,* described our own trading styles and techniques. In *Electronic Day Traders' Secrets,* we went straight to some of the best traders we have been privileged to work with, who have either taken a course through George West's company, Tradersedge.net, formerly Broadway Consulting, or been customers of Marc Friedfertig's brokerage firm, Broadway Trading, LLC. These traders have described what has worked for them.

This book would not be complete without providing some insight into what separates traders who succeed from those who don't. All of the traders you have read about here have been successful because of their ability to capitalize on opportunities to profit while minimizing the potential for losses—something that many traders tend to lose sight of.

Timing and Discipline

Successful trading is more than making winning trades. It comes down to two ratios. The first ratio is the percentage of winning trades to the percentage of losing trades. The second ratio is the amount traders make when they are right to what they lose when they are wrong. These factors ultimately determine success.

The first ratio is dependent on timing. Some of the traders in this book emphasized knowing a stock's levels; others referred to instinct, gut feel, or waves. One deemed it seasoned judgment, while others credited momentum and relative strength. All of these methods share a common thread: timing. Timing can profoundly influence your ratio of winners to losers.

The ability to pick winners can be addicting, and many traders spend their entire careers obsessed with timing. They watch charts, relative strength, formulas, or news, or they just read the tape. Tape reading is a practiced art, described in Edwin Lefevre's 1923 investment classic *Reminiscences of a Stock Operator* (Wiley, 1994). Modern-day tape readers combine relative strength and the market-maker techniques such as those outlined in *The Electronic Day Trader.* Charting, technical analysis, and timing techniques are described in numerous other books and online services. But timing is only one part of the trade. A more important skill is discipline.

Discipline is the second key to successful trading. It is the fundamental element that will determine how much you make and how much you lose. Finding winners, however—a matter of good timing—is much more fun than taking losses or selling out winners, which requires strong discipline. And in fact, that's why many traders fail. The experience of thousands of day traders demonstrates that timing, while critical to a trader's psyche, is only as good as the discipline that will help the trader book profits and cut losses. If a trader does not develop a high degree of discipline, it doesn't matter how good the timing is, because discipline is what will keep the trader in the game over the long run.

Of course, many traders and would-be traders spend far more time trying to pick winners than they do worrying about their losers. Certainly it's more exciting to enter a trade in anticipation of potential gains than to exit a trade to cut a loss. As one day trader noted, "Any number of traders can enter a good trade. The best traders know how to exit, but not out of necessity." These traders recognize that in the long run they will prosper by selling when they can—not when they have to. And while they press their winners, they also know when to take profits.

Is this the result of discipline, timing, or perhaps a bit of both? It's discipline. A disciplined trader does not allow winners to become losers, and discipline ultimately leads to prudent selling when greed screams, "Push harder." Most important, it is discipline that forces traders to control their losses. Timing gets them into the trade, but discipline gets them out. Timing determines how often they are right or wrong, but discipline controls how much they will make or lose. Therefore, discipline ultimately decides a trader's success or failure.

Money Management

When successful traders talk about discipline they really are referring to *money management*. Many view discipline only as a tool for controlling losses, but a successful trader also needs to have discipline in controlling profits. Money management involves both—or perhaps it is better to say that money management encompasses managing both your winning trades and your losing trades. Good money management will determine what you make versus the amount you lose. Money management is reflected in your average gain per trade or ticket average, and it is money management—not timing—that is most crucial to success. A trader with poor timing but adroit money management skills still has a good chance to succeed. But the odds are against a trader with great timing and second-rate money management ability. Yet it is timing with which most traders are obsessed.

Traders are constantly searching for a secret formula which will give them the timing they believe is so crucial for success. They devour books, charts, and lessons on technical analysis. The best traders come to realize that there is no magic bullet, no Holy Grail. Timing can only target a potential entry point. Money management is the main ingredient in any trading strategy, because it, above all, determines whether you will make money.

One of the key elements to successful money management is establishing a personal set of rules and adhering to them. Having had the opportunity to train and work with thousands of day traders, we can tell you with certainty that the number one reason new traders fail or lose money is that they do not control their losses. The idea of controlling losses is relatively simple: create parameters defining what you are willing to risk—and stick to them. Unfortunately, for most traders this is more easily said than done. Most people do not follow their own rules because no rules work all the time. Traders create rules and then tend to change them as each trading episode ends differently.

For example, say that you pick a risk level of half a point. You buy a stock, and it goes half a point against you, so you think about your rules and whether you should sell the stock. The reality is that sometimes the stock is going to continue to go lower and other times it will bounce back. People tend to remember the times the stock bounced back and proved them right, but let's say that you sell the stock for a half a point loss, and the next thing you know, the stock is $2 higher. What will you think the next time a stock moves half a point against you? If you are like most people, you will be tempted to hold it, knowing that there is a chance that the stock will go back up. Before you know it, that stock has moved a point and a half against you. The positive reinforcement of being proved right was far more influential than having to admit that you were wrong.

Good discipline can make all the difference. When traders find themselves being "whipsawed," it is usually their timing that is getting them in at the wrong point. Timing, however, is not responsible for getting them out—discipline is. Bad timing can necessitate discipline and can also force traders to second-guess their rules. The best traders will employ both good timing and good discipline. Poor traders are simply those without discipline. Bad timing initially gets them into trouble, and bad discipline shows them the door.

The solution to this is to separate your rules into two categories: rules that work more often than they fail and rules that keep you in business. The ultimate goal of your rules is to ensure that you manage your money successfully. While some traders may argue that there are times to break the rules and take risks outside of your money management procedures, most traders who are in for the long haul will counter that you must never break the rules designed to keep you in business.

Following are a few basic rules that we believe have the most profound impact on whether a trader will be successful—or perhaps should find another line of work.

Controlling Losses

Rule #1: Limit Your Risk in Any Trade

The concept is quite simple: when you enter a trade, decide how much you are willing to risk. Pick a dollar figure that equals some percentage of the amount you would expect to make on a successful trade. The two-to-one concept might be a fair guide. If you think that you should make ¾ of a point on a winning trade, for instance, don't risk more than half of this—⅜—on a loser. It doesn't take a genius to figure out that if you are making less money on winners than on losers, you will not be around the trading room for very long.

Most important, you must stick to whatever amount you decide to risk. If you find yourself frequently being stopped out and forced to exit a trade, you may need to work on timing or give your trades more leeway. Adjust this risk parameter over time to fit your style, but not with every trade or day to day. It's also critical to determine how much you are willing to risk through different time periods. Know what you are willing to risk for any given day, week, or month, and stick to it. New traders might even consider defining how much they are willing to risk over their careers.

If you are considering day trading, or even if you are an experienced trader attempting electronic day trading for the first time, you must try to be conservative with the amount you risk. Even if you are well off, losing money is no fun and only puts you deeper in the hole. As a new electronic day trader, it is essential to avoid increasing risk until you have established a profitable track record. So trade conservatively while you're learning. Until you know the ropes and develop a strategy, it's easier—and smarter—to day trade 100 shares of Apple Computer, a medium-priced, low-volatility stock, than to blaze through 1000 shares of high-priced, highly volatile Amazon.com.

Rule #2: Know When to Get Smaller

Here's another rule that's more easily said than done: if the trades are not going well, get smaller. Unfortunately, people tend to do just the opposite. Many traders push harder when they're down, hoping to make up the loss—and maybe even score a win—with a powerful late-inning home run. It's the mind-set of gamblers who are losing big-time playing $20-a-hand blackjack. Down on their luck and thoroughly dejected, they slouch over to the roulette table and bet their last $2000 on red—hoping to win everything back in one shot. Sometimes they get lucky. But if they repeat this gamble time and again, chances are that one morning they'll wake up with a hangover and an empty wallet. That's no way to day trade. If you're not making money, get smaller. Reduce your risk immediately and wait for a better opportunity. No trader should ever be ashamed to decrease their trading size. Big egos have ended many trading careers.

If you tumble into a rut, there are several essential steps toward getting back on track:

- *Stop the bleeding.*   Get out of losers and cut the amount of shares you trade.
- *Step aside.*   Analyze what you may be doing wrong. Are you fighting the trend or getting hit with big losses?

Perhaps your timing is poor. Are you trading without a game plan, or don't know which price levels your stocks are coming from? Any one of these factors can quickly break a trader.

- *Get back to basics.* Try to get even again by trading small share-lots. Tough as it is, you must mentally prepare yourself for a long road ahead. Traders who want to recoup their losses in one trade, or even one day, usually end up striking out. Take it one step at a time. Choke up on the bat and just try and hit a few singles to get your confidence back. The doubles and triples will take care of themselves. If all else fails, consider taking a break from trading to clear your head.

  Good traders always go back to the basics when they are losing; great traders stick to them no matter what. *This game can be deceptively simple. Press when things are going well; take profits when you can, not when you have to; don't let winners turn into losers; and get smaller when you are losing.* If you can make money, don't give it back. Getting smaller when things are not going your way is key to being in this business for the long run.

Rule #3: Ease In and Ease Out

Good quarterbacks will adapt throughout a game by recognizing the opposition's weaknesses. They instantly evaluate their teams' needs and aren't afraid to throw the ball away if that's their best option. Similarly, good traders analyze the trading day as it progresses. Are their trades working? Can they sell on the offer? What is their goal for the day? Good traders follow the money flows and notice the market's subtle hints. They know to become selective and stick to the game plan when the going gets tough—as it inevitably does. Just like quarterbacks, good traders must ease into and out of positions and situations. They don't throw the long bomb on every play—they are judicious. By developing a feel for the market, traders can learn when to go for a score and when to punt.

Start slowly. Buy one stock. If the market is going your way, consider buying another. If the trades are going well, keep on. If conditions start to change, you have to shift accordingly. The morning was great; you made several profitable trades and had just a few losers. But your last three trades didn't go anywhere. This is a signal to become selective and reevaluate your situation. Slow down. Consider trading smaller. As the afternoon progresses and the trend appears to resume, consider stepping up the pace. But evaluate each step as if it was your first. Understand what works and what doesn't, and structure your trading accordingly.

Good traders ease into positions. As your career progresses and you consider trading larger and larger positions, this rule will become vital to your money management. If you like a stock, you don't have to put all your money to work at once. Buy 1000 shares. If it goes your way, consider buying another 1000. If it continues, add another 1000. It's not necessary—or wise—to push your limit in one shot. Remember, ease in, ease out. In this way, you're apt to make more than you lose.

Rule #4: Never Double up on a Losing Position

This is a hard rule to follow, but it will keep you in business. You sit down at a table in a casino, bet $10, and lose. You bet $20, and lose again. You bet $30; it's gone, too. Then, desperate, you put down 60 bucks and you win. You're even again.

And you're also lucky. Doubling up on losers is a recipe for going broke. Add to winners. Dump losers.

If, after all the warnings, you still feel compelled to double up on losing positions, then you must set new risk parameters and stick to them. For instance, say a stock goes a dollar against you and you had originally planned to risk only a half. Yet the reason for entering the trade is still intact and you believe the stock will recover. So you buy another lot. At this point, you must mentally establish a line in the sand for at least the second lot—and probably for the entire position. You must tell yourself, "I know I shouldn't be doing this, so if the stock goes down another ¼, I will sell my second lot. If the stock goes down still another ¼, I will sell the rest." This mindset is the only way to stay in the game over the long run. If you flaunt this rule, or even worse, double up again as the original stake goes further against you, it won't be long before your trading career self-destructs.

Rule #5: No Overnight Losers

You want to go home every night with a clean slate. We strongly advocate closing out any losing positions at the end of the day, particularly for new traders. Stop your losing streak at one. Don't get married to a position. Tomorrow is another day and there is always another opportunity. Don't let one bad trade ruin your day—or your career.

The problem with taking home losers is they usually turn into bigger dogs the following morning. This will not only get your brain thinking about breaking other rules, but it will distract you from the game plan you would have implemented had you come to work flat. In addition, most people who take home losers are praying that they will open in their favor the next day. If you ever find yourself hoping and praying, chances are that you are already beat.

Day trading has no room for stubbornness. Don't justify a losing position. Frankly, the first step to making money is to stop losing money. Treat this as a hard-and-fast rule and you stand a good chance to win in the long run.

The number one reason day traders fail is that they don't control their losses. These rules are designed to help you avoid that trap. Of course, no rule works all the time, and rules are only as good as the discipline you give them. Know your limits. Trade the way you feel most comfortable. And keep control. For if you can control losses, controlling profits should take care of itself.

Controlling Profits

Skillful money management also requires controlling profits. It's a sad fact of trading life that great successes are often followed by great failures. Many traders get carried away with the excitement of a big trade or a big day. They will press when the time is right and get bigger when things are going well, just as they have been taught. But then they watch helplessly as their precious profits drain away when things are not going their way.

Making money is not the same as keeping it. Traders who lack good money management skills often fail to recognize when their situation changes and it's time to get smaller. When they are up $1000, they want to make $2000. When they are up $2000, they want to make $5000. When they are up $5000, they must make $10,000. Then, when they give back $2000 and they are up only $3000, all they can think about is getting back to that magical $5000. Greed makes them vulnerable, and they will press even though they have begun to do poorly. They will break rules that they have set for themselves in an attempt to regain lost ground. In this mad dash for dollars, most will erase what profits they have left and may even fall into negative territory. They push their luck until it runs out.

Here are some ideas to help you control profits—a vital part of day-trading success.

Ease In, Ease Out

Just as you ease into positions in controlling losses, you do the same when controlling profits. With every step, day traders must evaluate what works and what doesn't. Of course, traders should add to their winners. Certainly traders should be more aggressive when things are going well. But traders also must know when to pull back. Watch the market trend. Pay attention to your own results. If you start to give back profits, slow down. Be very selective. In short, if your winning technique is losing its luster, cut back.

Know When to Get Bigger

There is no reason to get bigger—to trade larger share-lots—until you are making money. Getting bigger should come naturally with experience. As you progress, you should gradually add to the size of your trades. But always remember that there is no shame in getting smaller. Even the most successful traders take a step back sometimes. If an obvious trend appears or you notice that other traders are having a strong day, you might decide to increase your trading size. Clearly, the most important factor in determining when to trade larger size is your own performance. If you are doing well, get bigger. If not, downsize quickly.

Set Goals

Another important element in controlling profits is setting goals: daily, weekly, and monthly. These goals can help keep a trader disciplined.

Most people have a level of income that they find comfortable. This is not how much they hope to make; it's not even the amount they need to get by. This is a level that they are subconsciously willing to accept. Interestingly, when people are below this comfort level, many will do whatever it takes to reach it. Even more curious is that when people make more money than their predetermined comfort level, especially those paid by performance, such as salespeople and traders, they tend to drift back down to their comfort zone. But the most successful salespeople overcome this natural bias and continue to achieve the best results they can—even after they have achieved what was originally expected of them. Traders need to set similar goals.

New day traders should consider a break-even goal. Day traders who consistently hurdle their stated goals might consider raising the bar. Traders who track their results should be able to improve performance by focusing on what matters most—the profit and loss statement after the closing bell. Set higher goals in small increments that can ultimately lead to a greater and more satisfying end result. Modest daily goals can add up to big year-end numbers. Clearing $200 each day over roughly 250 trading days adds up to $50,000 a year; $1000 a day equals $250,000 a year. Try for consistency. Hitting singles regularly, traders are more likely to exceed their expectations, while eliminating large swings in both profits and losses.

Keep What You Earn

Traders who keep goal sheets are frequently confused by what to do once they reach their goal during the trading day. Do you lock in profits or get bigger because you're trading well? Is it possible to do both?

The answer is simple: If you reach your goal, don't stop trading. If you stop, you will never discover your true potential. You may miss out on a day that offers unusual activity and opportunities. Instead of stopping immediately, consider completing one more trade that you believe has a high probability of success and a small degree of risk. If you make money on the trade, consider another.

If ever a trade does not work out, reassess your situation. Do not risk all of your gains. As a general guideline we suggest that you risk 20 percent of your profits to take advantage of a unique day and to test your mettle. But be sure to walk away a winner. It is essential that you are particularly conservative when you make that one additional trade. And if you trade after you've attained your daily goal, don't lose sight of the big picture. Above all, keep your profit.

Other Goals

Traders may also want to set goals to help them stick to their strategy, such as "I will not violate my rules." Give yourself a target and you may be surprised at how well you can aim.

Wall Street Is Not Easy Street

What makes a trader successful? What makes a trader unsuccessful? Do I book profits or press my winners? Do I try to control emotions or can I rely on instinct?

Perhaps it comes as no surprise that contradictions surface in a book that encompasses many different strategies, theories, and personalities. But the commonality among the traders in this book is encouraging, while the few contradictions can be valuable lessons.

Most of these traders were quick to admit that their success did not come easily. Their long, hard road was an intensive and expensive life lesson that many traders do not survive. These traders defied the odds and flourished from fundamental shifts in the marketplace. These traders have been consistently profitable and have earned far more than most, with the exception of professional athletes or entertainers. And like many athletes and entertainers, these traders appear to have a true passion for their work.

But a trader's skills and talent, unlike a performer's or an athlete's, are hardly a rare gift. Honestly, it's difficult to argue that successful day traders have distinct talents, skills, or qualities that set them apart from anyone else. Most of these traders started out just like many of you who are now reading this book. If they have any unique quality at all, it's that they allowed themselves to learn from their experiences and mistakes. They learned from their trades, from the market, and from other traders. Even now, they do not allow their egos to build them up or bring them down. They accept failures and refuse to gloat over success. In fact, considering their accomplishments, they are remarkably modest. At the same time, they are supremely confident—not necessarily in their ability to pick stocks but in their adaptability to changes in the market.

Many day traders speak of an extreme level of concentration or focus that some call the "zone." To be sure, extreme concentration is an attribute of most successful people. Their love for their work helps them to elevate their focus to a high level. As for their trading, most of the traders interviewed stay with the trend, go where the action is, and react swiftly and appropriately to market swings. They press their winners, yet recognize that it's a game of singles hitters. They don't try to buy the bottom or sell the top, but rather ease into and out of positions. Some point out that a good exit strategy—when you sell—is even more important than when you buy. Many alluded to playing a stock's relative strength, but recognized the wisdom of buying pullbacks and not chasing stocks higher. Most important, many reiterated the fundamental rule of selling when you can, not when you have to.

Before You Trade

Consistency in day trading will come from sticking to a money management plan. The market can be extremely humbling. Many traders take all the credit when they are successful and blame the market when they are not. The reality is that, with few exceptions, your trades will never really change the market. Your 1000 shares of Intel have almost nothing to do with the stock's next move. The market will function with you or without you. It doesn't matter if you made millions for the last 10 years straight—it is essential to define what you are willing to risk now and stick with it. The main reason that most traders fail after great successes is that their egos drag them down. They get full of themselves. The only antidote is for traders to stick to their rules and be disciplined.

For those of you who may consider entering this exciting field, be smart. The best advice is often the simplest. At the outset, define how much you are willing to risk—in other words, what you can stand to lose. Begin trading conservatively and work hard to preserve your capital while you learn. Trade 100-share lots, avoid highflyers, and learn as much as you can for the least amount of risk.

If you do plan to day trade for a living, it's recommended that you start with at least $75,000. We suggest that you risk $15,000—or 20 percent—and give the process six months during which you can decide whether day trading is viable for you.

With this in mind, do not risk more than $5000 in any month, $2000 in any week, or $500 in any day. These numbers do not add up exactly, but you probably won't lose the maximum every day, every week, and every month. You are likely to have some winning trades and some profitable days. And as your timing and money management improve, you should have profitable weeks and then months. As your profits grow, you may consider increasing the size of your trades as long as you stick to the same structure. In time, as you prove you can make money and you increase your size, you will have to assume more risk. If you risked a quarter on your 100-share trades, you should still risk only a quarter on your 1000-share trades. Increasing the number of shares you trade will heighten your risk. But do not risk more in a day, week, or month than you generally make, so don't lose $5000 on a bad day if you make only $1500 on a good day.

Developing the Trader's Edge

Electronic Day Traders' Secrets was written to give you insights from individuals who represent a few of the industry's best electronic day traders. We hope this book has provided you with an idea of what it's like to day trade for a living. It's clear that while successful day traders truly seem to enjoy their work, none describes it as easy. Day trading for a living is serious business—and anyone who sees it otherwise is likely to trade at a severe disadvantage. New traders should start small, taking as little risk as possible until they have proven they can deliver consistent results. The first step to profitable trading is to stop losing. There is no reason to trade more than the minimum 100 shares until you have concrete reasons to believe that you can be profitable at day trading. Day trading can be extremely humbling and traders are never too experienced to reduce the size of their positions when stocks go against them.

While there are risks to day trading, there is risk anytime you start your own business. This book should prove valuable for those who want to give day trading a chance and for those who already day trade. If you become a day trader, remember that trading is a continual learning experience even for the best. You must continue to read, grow, and learn. Learn from other traders, such as those in this book. But most of all, learn from your own experiences.

Today, individual traders can be on a level playing field with Wall Street professionals. Fast, low-cost executions, instant access to information, technological advancements, and a favorable regulatory environment have made it possible for individuals to trade stocks with the same tools that the market makers use. Wall Street's insurmountable advantage is history. Most successful day traders are well trained, with the best technology and ample capital. It is now possible for individuals to obtain the necessary skills and software to earn consistent returns that were previously available only to the Wall Street elite.

Your decision to read this book demonstrates an effort to learn about day trading. Many of the traders interviewed in this book described trading as an ongoing learning experience. We believe that the concepts and thoughts conveyed through these interviews provide a solid foundation for any trader. Day trading, like most entrepreneurial ventures, requires hard work, persistence, and resilience. And it does not come easily. Those who conquer these challenges and succeed will say that day trading is one of the best jobs in the world. We hope that we have provided you with realistic expectations regarding what it takes to become a successful day trader, as well as insight into how some of the best in the business capitalize on the opportunities that can be found in today's dynamic trading environment.

Good luck!

Index

About the Authors

Marc Friedfertig has trained thousands of day traders to cut out the middle people and earn superior returns trading options, listed securities, and NASDAQ stocks. Mr. Friedfertig is the coauthor of *The Electronic Day Trader*, a best-selling book, and is the managing member of Broadway Trading, LLC (www.broadwaytrading.com), a brokerage firm that specializes in electronic day trading. His firm, Broadway Trading, is one of the leading firms in the industry. Broadway typically executes more than 30,000 transactions a day.

Prior to founding Broadway Trading, Mr. Friedfertig was a member of the American Stock Exchange for eight years, where he supervised and trained traders and was himself one of the top traders. He has also traded index futures as well as day traded electronically from off the floor. Mr. Friedfertig earned his MBA at Columbia University. Mr. Friedfertig is regularly quoted in national newspapers and magazines as well as on the radio and television.

George West is an active day trader and president of Tradersedge.net (previously known as Broadway Consulting Group). Tradersedge.net is a leading provider of day-trading services, including books, videos, seminars, and online chat rooms. Tradersedge.net has succeeded in training hundreds of traders from a wide variety of professional backgrounds. Previously, he traded stocks and options on major exchanges and was an option market maker on the American Stock Exchange. While a trader with Spear Leeds & Kellogg, he handled order flow of large institutional investors. He graduated from St. Lawrence University and was coauthor with Marc Friedfertig of *The Electronic Day Trader*.

Jonathan Burton writes about investing and business for many publications, including *Bloomberg Personal Finance*, *Individual Investor*, and *Mutual Funds*. His in-depth interviews with leading financial-industry figures appear regularly in *Dow Jones Asset Management*. He has been a senior writer at *Worth* and a correspondent for *The Far Eastern Economic Review*.